A common sense addiction ~~recovery~~
discovery book
for all those affected by their own addictions
or the addictions of others

ADDICTION
UNPLUGGED
HOW TO BE FREE

Read it. Live it. Share its liberating message.

JOHN FLAHERTY

Balboa Press books may be ordered through booksellers or by contacting:

Balboa Press
A Division of Hay House
1663 Liberty Drive
Bloomington, IN 47403
www.balboapress.com
1 (877) 407-4847

Printed in the United States of America.

ISBN: 978-1-4525-8938-1 (sc)
ISBN: 978-1-4525-8940-4 (hc)
ISBN: 978-1-4525-8939-8 (e)

Library of Congress Control Number: 2013923780

Balboa Press rev. date: 01/17/2014

BALBOA.
PRESS
A DIVISION OF HAY HOUSE

Dedicated to bringing freedom to humanity:
We are so much greater than our thoughts would have us *think* we are!

CONTENTS

A human being is part of the whole, called by us "universe";
a part limited in time and space.
He experiences himself, his thoughts and feelings as
something separated from the rest--a kind of optical
delusion of his consciousness.

Albert Einstein

We can all hand over our lives to some-one or to some-thing. As soon as we do this, we give to that someone or that something, a power and an authority over us which diminishes our individuality and depletes us of energy.

You have been doing precisely that with your life. It is why you have been relying so heavily on drugs, alcohol or other addictive behaviors to sustain you. The fact that you are now in possession of this book is your indication that you have either exhausted that particular dependency, taken it as far as you can, or, that your dependency has exhausted you! Either way, life is inviting you to make the personal transformation your heart has always desired for you. I know that to be true from my own life experience.

In the past, I handed over much of my life to other people and to other things, similarly depleting my own personal energy, until I reached the point of physical, mental, emotional and spiritual "break-down". The more I continued trying to live my life for an authority, the less I felt charged to be an effective presence in my life. The authority I handed my individuality over to was the Roman Catholic Church. I entered the seminary at the age of 11 years old and was ordained a Catholic Priest at the age of 24, going on to serve in the priestly ministry for 11 years. At the time of my greatest need, however, I was "sold out" by the very authority I had pledged my life to and sacrificed my life for. Only with the gift of hindsight and after many years of deep personal pain, do I now fully realize that my life had never been *my* life at all. I had handed my life over to the ownership of the Church and my every expression became a suppression. I was programmed, coerced, conditioned and groomed to uphold the

Church's public face at the expense of my own state of heart and mind. I was on the brink of self-annihilation; mentally, physically, spiritually and emotionally drained. It is only today, at a distance of 30 years since my admission to the priesthood, that I am capable of seeing just how much that way of living was squeezing me of life and rendering me power-less.

While I recognize that the priesthood is the source of great joy for some, it was not the path that was ever going to bring freedom to my heart which had become saddened, abused and depleted of natural joy. In the absence of natural joy, I increasingly looked to external things to sustain me, just as you have done with your addictions. My heart yearned for a sense of completeness, but the "way" of my life seemed to block all possibilities for me to experience it. I felt imprisoned by life itself and became rooted in a victim mentality of utter helplessness.

The Church's requirement of a priest is to sacrifice his life for the growth of that Church; to live in devotion to God in service of it with an "undivided heart". Yet, for me, the opposite was my experience. The more I tried to serve those in my care and fulfill my role as a stimulus for growth and reflection, the more I was restricted. I felt stunted by an authority with its tradition, its dogmas, its beliefs (judgments), its theories and its fixed and external set of rules.

My situation was a paradigm of conflict: the more I tried to assist an individual's desire to make personal transformation and spiritual growth within those confines, the more my own heart was becoming "divided." I know now that personal transformation and spiritual growth cannot depend simply on a static and external set of rules. Life cannot be harnessed, suppressed and controlled this way. Something had to "give" and after much heartache, considerable confusion and deep pain, it finally dawned that the some-thing to be changed in my life was the authority to which I had given such power.

Once the function of an authority is reduced to being repressive, it loses its persuasiveness as an educator. The consequence of such repression is the formation of people who are inept and without motivation. I had become inept, lost, without motivation or purpose. I no longer felt alive. I felt like I was dying to live. If a conscience struggles between what it wants to be and what it really is by its tendencies, inclinations and promptings, there must be room for freedom of inquiry and expression. Without it, there is always conflict. I am well aware that there are any number of priests who "think" differently from the official canons of the Church. However, it is more difficult to find one who expresses his thought openly, without running into difficulties with authority. Increasingly, the hand that was feeding me was fast becoming the hand that was depleting me. Whenever ideology collides with daily existence, further tensions are always created. When those tensions reached their maxim in me, my life as I had known it began to disintegrate.

We rarely make life-changing decisions by gentle reminders alone, particularly when we have literally spent a life-time adhering to someone or to something we have given our personal power to. Life often has to take over, when we feel inept or unmotivated to do so. When it does, it may have to pull the rug from underneath our feet, in order to fully get our attention and wake us up to the wider implications of our earlier decisions. We can make life-changes the hard way or the easy way. Until we become more consciously aware that there always is an easier way, the harder way is inevitably thought to be our only option.

In my case, my life had to unceremoniously fall apart before it could be put back together. While at the time it seemed like the worst experience of my life, it has since proved to be the most liberating and the most transformative. Life is always conspiring in our favor. That freeing discovery is the foundation of this book and has been the basis of my teaching since that time. More significantly for me, it marked the time of removing myself from victim consciousness and the beginning of Self awareness, Self discovery and Self empowerment. I began to get to the very core of my Being, a discovery that opened the way to my life's true purpose; loving myself back to life.

My work since those years has been dedicated to assisting hundreds of people across the globe to reclaim their spiritual power, to be their own authority and to discover how to be free. Ironically enough, the powerful Christ message, which ultimately is a message of personal freedom, has now been more possible for me to share with others, without the restriction placed on it by religious interpretation and doctrinal ownership. It was, not surprisingly, relatively easy for me to make the transition from being a teacher of spirituality within the Church to teaching the way of freedom to those hungering for their true identity and purpose; those in addiction.

As you read the chapters of this book, you'll find that it is very different to the regular addiction recovery books. It is not a book to entertain the intellect. It is not a book written to convince you of the merits of being free of your addictions or dependencies. Rather, it is a book primarily written to remind you of the truth of who you are. You will come to that truth, as I did, by first of all discovering all you are NOT. Once you become more conscious of your Being, your awareness expands. The "world" you were introduced to, and the "role" you were taught to play out can be seen through a new lens and lived in an entirely different way. Your life literally becomes *your* life. Who you have learned to think you are and who you learned to think other people think you are, makes way for the truth of the all that you are.

The message of this book is profound in its simplicity:
As Your Conscious Awareness Expands, Addictions Dissolve.

It is a common sense "discovery" book, written for you and about you. The only trouble with common sense is ... it's not very common! You'll need to do some inner exploration of your own Being to make sense of your Self and I will be sharing with you some practical ways for you to do that.

The purpose of this book: your freedom

Freedom is not worth having if it does not include the freedom to make mistakes

—Mahatma Gandhi

Life is making an invitation to you right here and right now through the pages of this book, the first addiction *discovery* book of its kind. The invitation life is making, is for you to discover who you truly are. Yes, that's right, for you to know who you are, what you're about, what life's about and what your place is in it.

Unlike the more regular addiction *recovery* books, this is written so you may *discover* everything your heart has always been looking for. It's about all that's right with you, all that's genuine about you, all that's true about you, all that's totally understandable about you. Things you have forgotten to re-member about YOU.

There is not a doubt in my mind, after working in the field of addiction for more than 25 years, that conventional approaches to *recovery*, while assisting you to make many adjustments, still fail to open up to you what you are missing most. Everywhere I go, I find people who are calling out from the deepest part of their Being for a more complete and fulfilling experience of themselves. They have often been using alcohol and prescribed or un-prescribed substances in the absence of the very experience for which their heart yearns; a new definition of themselves and a new meaning.

The pages of this book are written to assist you in defining and living the grander experience of your Self that you have been seeking. In building a life deeply aligned with your purpose, you will come to a new and powerful understanding of your Self and specifically, you will discover how to be free.

The first thing to acknowledge is that your life is only your life as you've been living it. It's only how you've been making sense of it, how you have learned to piece it together. The meaning of your life is the meaning you have given to it and for as long as that meaning has gone unquestioned by you, it has gone unchanged. Your life is the experience of yourself you have come to believe is YOU. If your experience of life is working perfectly well, then you may have no reason to alter it. If it has not been working for you, you are about to discover how to experience your life from a completely different starting place and with a whole new meaning. You can do that for you. In fact, there's only you that can do that for you. That's how powerful you are!

You may well wonder where the meaning you have been giving to your own life ever came from in the first place. Did you really decide to conjure up such an unfulfilling one? Or did you give your life that meaning without really meaning it?

Your experience of addiction, like some of your other experiences, will have genuinely been your earnest attempt to look for more, more of YOU. You have been searching over a very long time for more than that which you'd *pieced together* about life and about yourself. The longer it has taken, the more frustrating it will have been. Accept your frustration. It is not a fault that you are frustrated; it is a truth. Life will always be frustrating for as long as the one thing missing most from it is YOU!

Your addictive behaviors are reminders. That's all they are. They are reminders of the *more*, you haven't yet found. You have been searching for YOU, for your very Being. It's not that you don't know who you are, but you have forgotten to re-member how to be the *all* that you are. You have forgotten that you are Infinite Consciousness, pure potential.

The various twists and turns of life, and the role you have learned to play in it have all been instrumental in your forgetfulness. Your addictive behaviors were part and parcel of that. Yet, oddly enough, they've also been part and parcel of your deep desire to find YOU. That's why it's been hard to know the most advantageous route to take. You've been trying to disentangle your Self from the fantasy you originally made up about yourself, without even knowing that that has been causing your frustration.

Now you hold in your hands a book that reminds you how to bring your efforts to completion, how to give yourself back to your Self and how to live your life without the frustration you've been experiencing. That's how powerful the message of this book is!

It's now time to let your life be this message and to let the expansion of this message be your life.

Remember, it has taken each of your experiences, without exception, to bring you to greater awareness. Don't stop off at faulting your past and blaming yourself or anyone else for those times. It's just that you now feel more ready to make the radical change you desire and life is moving you on to realize it. You are about to bring a totally new you into existence and already a new meaning and a newly defined purpose is unfolding. If that were not so, this book wouldn't have made its way into your hands, nor would you be ready to receive its message; but it has and you are.

It is my desire for you, that your own desire for yourself at last becomes your own experience. Then you will feel your re-alignment with life itself. You might say that life would then be your own again, and indeed it is.

You have spent long enough being out of alignment, now I am going to show you the short cut to being true to your Self again. It is how to be free, and I know you are more than ready for that.

CHAPTER ONE

Discovering how powerful you are

Everybody is a genius. But if you judge a fish by its ability to climb a tree, it will live its whole life believing it is stupid.

–Albert Einstein

I encourage you to read *Addiction Unplugged : How To Be Free* very carefully with a mind that is wide open to having many of your cherished beliefs challenged about addiction, about recovery and indeed about life itself. You would do well to begin by giving yourself the *permission slip* to un-know everything about addiction that you have come to know.

You would also do well to un-learn everything you have come to learn about life—your life— as you have come to understand it. Even put to one side what you may call the *common sense* things, which often enough, are little more than handed down judgments about life, rather than truths. Take a deep breath, and like magic, go ahead now ... un-know and un-learn ...

There, it wasn't too difficult was it? After all, you've never really believed all that known and learned stuff anyway, have you? If you had, then your life would have been working just nicely by now, wouldn't it? The fact that it isn't, can really boil down to only one thing: how you have learned to make sense of your world feels all upside down and ... always has.

... as long as you keep trying to make someone else's version of your life take the place of your own definition, there will always be heartache.

The way you have been trying to make your life work may have been the way shown to you by your parents, partners, family, friends, teachers, counselors and others, but for you, there's still something missing. You are looking for YOU and for as long as you keep trying to make someone else's version of your life take the place of your own definition, there will always be heartache. So it's now time for you to discover how to exchange the *upside-down* world that was shown to you, and which you've been trying to live out ever since, for the more *right-way-up* world, that at last feels true to you.

The liberating message I am sharing here is a message for the frustrated seeker, and of course that is you. You may have read everything about addiction recovery (or think you have), been everywhere to seek help (or convinced yourself you have), tried every therapy to overcome your addictions (and told everyone you have), attended all kinds of treatments in pursuit of a cure (or seems like you have) and yet still feel stuck! Sometimes taking one step forward and always at least two back, you have absorbed all the information out there and yet never moved beyond the same starting place.

HEART AND HEAD. My intention for bringing this message to you is to explain why your experience of life has been the way it has been and to open up to you an entirely new way of experiencing it. My message to you is to take heart, for the answers to your challenges and the new experience you've been looking for are to be found not in your head, but in your heart. I also realize you will have to be taught how to be attuned to your heart because that won't have been shown to you before. Once it has, you will wonder how you ever missed it.

I remind you that your frustration at yourself for not knowing the way is no bad thing. It may not always feel nice to be frustrated, but frustration is the emotion that is indicating two things to pay attention to, so you may be free:

1. The solutions you have been looking for certainly exist. Your heart knows this, but until now, only your head has been consulted about the matter. Your head does not know all that there is to know. Your head can only give you information it has already been supplied with and the different starting place you are seeking is not amongst its supplies. In the absence of that *knowing*, you'll feel frustrated.

2. Your head has not accepted that it cannot provide you with the different starting place you have been looking for. It has only ever learned that what it doesn't know, is not worth knowing. You have settled for that, but your heart has not. Your heart is aware that what the head calls *different* actually means everything not known to it. Your heart has yet to be consulted about the matter. In the absence of that consultation, you'll feel frustrated.

The first thing to grasp and to accept about the addictions in your life is that they were learned (collected along the way) and stored as memory in your unconscious mind. They created a behavior (that you mistakenly came to think was you) and you are now ready to change that experience of yourself (meaning you would like to un-learn the behaviors that have made your life the way it has been). Let me reveal to you the first truth you need to bring into your awareness, so you may have the freedom you seek ...

You are infinitely greater than your thoughts would
otherwise have you THINK you are.
You are infinitely greater than your beliefs would otherwise have you
BELIEVE you are.
Just because you've got used to your beliefs,
you don't have to continue THINKING them.
Just because you've got used to your thoughts,
you don't have to continue BELIEVING them.

Isn't that a freeing discovery? I suggest you read that last paragraph again because it contains truths that are freeing and they are truths you've possibly not been aware of before. Go ahead now and re-read it. It describes the different starting place, from which comes a whole new way of looking at life, your life.

BELIEFS AND JUDGMENTS. Just because you had come to THINK of yourself from your old ways of looking at life, you don't have to BELIEVE it's the only way to experience your life.

Just because you have got used to your addictions being so central in your life, you can soon not be-having them. That's how powerful you are!

A belief is just another word for a judgment. Beliefs (judgments) always come from some place else. They were on someone else's lips, before you made them your own. Once you make them your own, it becomes harder to differentiate between you with the belief and you without it. Ask yourself now in terms of your addiction:

"How would it feel to be without the belief I'm believing about myself right now?"
Put another way, ask yourself:
"How would it feel to be without the judgment I'm making about myself right now?"
If it feels empowering to be without that belief, save your new discovery. If it feels disempowering, delete it.
That's how powerful you are!

LEARNED BEHAVIORS. Know this too ... not only can you select your very next thought and make it your preferred belief about yourself, you can even select your next emotion and how you feel about yourself.

I agree, life would have been a whole lot easier if someone had just told you that great truth at the beginning, but they didn't. If it's any comfort to you, no one told me either, but since I discovered the difference it makes, I have felt duty-bound to let others in on it too. It is why I have written this book. I am delivering this life-changing message to you so that you may also discover how to select your own preferred thoughts and how to choose your own preferred emotions. When you master your discovery, you will also feel motivated to share with others the freedom it brings. You will then be living your truth and that will feel so much more fulfilling than living your learned behaviors.

Don't forget to remember ... Before there was ever a time when you were in addiction, there was a time when you were not. Before there was ever a time when you did not know the truth of who you *are*, there was a time when you did. My effort here is to remind you not to forget to remember the truth of all that you are. Consciousness is the *all* that you are and as you remember this essential truth, everything changes! Nothing new needs to be learned, only to be remembered. From your place of remembering, your conscious awareness will expand and from your expansion, your limitations will dissolve. That's how powerful you are!

BEING NOT DOING. Transcending your addictions is not a task you learn to *do*. It's not a *doing* thing at all. You cannot DO happy, you can only BE happy. You cannot DO joyful, you can only BE joyful. You cannot DO peaceful, you can only BE peaceful. You cannot DO sober, you can only BE sober. You cannot DO free, you can only BE free. Transcending your addictions is not an intellectual exercise for the head to master, it's the restoration of truth which your heart will re-member. Transcending your addictions is a return from thinking yourself the *Do-er* of your life to *Being* at one with it. It is the process of giving yourself back to your Self. That is how to be free.

Can you imagine how different AA or NA meetings would be if a person felt empowered enough to share the truth about their Being, rather than their upside-down learned behaviors. The more *right-feeling-way-up* person might declare themselves like this:

"My name is _____ and I am infinitely greater than my thoughts would otherwise have me THINK I am."

Wow, that would be some meeting to attend wouldn't it? From that new-found truth about yourself, every kind of change is made possible. All you would need to do thereafter is not to forget to re-member it!

LAWS OF THE UNIVERSE. For a time of course it will be easy to forget to remember the truth of your own power. I mean, just think how long it takes some people to profess how power-less they have become. There are people all over the world professing that they are power-less against drugs or alcohol, and, for as long as they make that their belief, it will indeed remain their experience. The "laws" of the universe will see to that. It's just the way the universe works.

> ... you are infinitely greater than who you have learned to become.

Now, I'm aware that there are many universal laws and truths that haven't been explained to you either, have they? In fact they aren't understood by many people. No wonder life can seem such an uphill struggle. However, all that is about to change for you.

As you go from chapter to chapter, I'll be introducing you to some of the key laws that could change everything; things about your addictions and things about life, your life. From this point on, simply be consciously aware, that you are infinitely greater than who you have learned to become.

CHAPTER TWO

There's so much more to YOU than you

There is a place that you are to fill and no-one else can fill, something you are to do, which no-one else can do.

—Florence Scovel Shinn

This is such an exciting time that you have reached in your life. It is also ironic. For oddly enough, it has taken your addictions to bring you to this place of discovery. Yes, it's taken your most unwanted experiences to bring you to your most wanted experience. Life is just like that and that is why it is unnecessary for you to spend time faulting your past or blaming others for your experiences. It is sufficient to simply be aware of them and to be aware of the thoughts and emotions that are associated with them. Judgment is not required.

Everyone discovers differently and your addictions have now done their job. They have been there to remind you of who you are NOT. It has taken time for you to first of all experience your *upside-down* version of life before you could next discover how to place it the *right-feeling-way-up*. Now you are becoming aware that you can do that.

As well as your addictive behaviors, there are many other things that also remind you of who you are NOT. You have not been able to identify them before because they had not been brought into your conscious awareness, but now they are and so now you can. That's how powerful you are!

> ... you are so much more than who you have come to THINK you are and so much more than who you have come to THINK other people THINK you are.

ALL YOU ARE NOT. You are not your thoughts, you are not your beliefs. You *have* thoughts and you *have* beliefs. You are not your body, you *have* a body. You are not your mother, you are not your father, you have *had* the experience in your life of being parented. You are not hopeless, you are not a failure, you are not any of the things you have learned to become. You are more powerful than the victim mentality you have settled for and the manipulative behavior you have become so skilled at. You are so much more than who you have come to THINK you are and so much more than who you have come to THINK other people THINK you are.

Only after sifting out all the things you are truly NOT, can you at last make the fulfilling *discovery* of all you truly are. From that discovery, you begin observing your life from an entirely different starting place to the one you have been trying to solve all your problems from before now. Until you received this message, you have been believing that you *are* your problems and that your challenges were far bigger than any solution to them. Why have you been doing that? Only because it's the way you were shown how to *do* life. It's the way you learned to understand and to experience everything.

You have been convincing yourself that there is life and then, quite separate from the rest of life, there is you. You have been living in the illusion of separateness, where everything can become a potential threat, where everything becomes that which has to be overcome. It is how you learned to fear and it is in fear that you have continued to make sense of your life. It is of course the way those who introduced you to life were trying to make sense of their own. You have just been following suit. You have not stopped to question, you have simply taken up from the same starting place that was given to you. In doing so, you have forgotten to re-member how to *be* in alignment with life itself.

THE STORY ABOUT YOU. You have been feeling like you are up against life, having to prove your worthiness of it. You have been unwittingly empowering your addictions and disempowering yourself. You have been magnifying your thoughts of lack and convincing yourself of unworthiness. You have been living the story created in your head about yourself over the truth known to your heart. You have been depressed about your past and living in anxiety that it will continue as your future. You have been living *who you thought you were*, or, *who other people thought you were*, while forgetting to re-member the truth of *all you are*. From that fear based belief, it's hardly surprising you would have reduced your life-choices down to one of only two possible options:

the constant repetition of a life-time in *addiction*
or
the unending experience of the need to be in *recovery*

It's quite possible that neither will sound very appealing to you. One may be more preferable to the other or less miserable than the other. Of course, many people find they slip from one into the other, this is known as "relapsing". However, my heart, like your heart, knows there must be more to life than this. And indeed, there is.

Try this experiment:

Cut your whole past away from you—no memory. You don't know who your parents are, you don't know to which country, religion or culture you belong. You don't know where you were brought up or where you were educated. Just cut the whole past.

Now, remembering how powerful you really are, speak out your newly discovered truths about yourself:

I am not my body
I am not my thoughts
I am not my mother
I am not my father
I am not a job
I am not a failure
I am not my addictions
I am not my recovery
I am not my judgments, nor the judgments made about me
I am not the I fantasy created about myself

And keep adding to the list as more of your new realizations come to you. When you are done, check in again with yourself ... You will find that your heart is still beating, your eyelids are still flickering, your pulse is pulsating, your breath is still breathing. You are still intact, without the need to keep in place anything else you had conjured up *about* yourself.

You *are*. Obviously you are. But *who* are you?
Having just cut the whole of your accumulated past away, you cannot feel an *I*. That is because there is no identity for you to associate with I, you have just cut it away, made it disappear.

Yet you are.

You are aware.
You have not disappeared.
You have not gone anywhere. Only what you had accumulated about you has gone, cut away.

Now, in the light of your new discovery, relax and breathe and become more consciously aware of all you truly *are*. You have just had your first experience of placing your own life the *right-feeling-way-up*.

YOUR NEW DISCOVERY. Savor your new discovery. See how good it feels. It will feel new to you of course, without carrying all that old accumulated *stuff* about you, but it's you! Always know ...

You are not and never can you be
separated from your Source

From your new discovery you can at last observe your life from an entirely different starting place. You have returned the *upside-down* world you have been trying to live out to its more *right-feeling-way-up*. Now I know you never thought you could do that, but you just have. It would only be someone else's judgment that could make you feel otherwise, but that is for you, not for anyone else to decide. That's how powerful you are!

Your questioning mind may well ask: "Isn't this just me going into denial?" Absolutely it is! It is part of your power to be in denial, but not in the way you have been taught to think of it.

Let me explain ...

With your life placed the *right-feeling-way-up*, you are making a complete denial of every untruth and judgment ever made about YOU. Doesn't that feel immensely freeing? Before today, you had never stopped to realize that the thoughts and beliefs you have been amassing about yourself are NOT your Self. As you start observing your life differently, you'll be able to see your collected thoughts and beliefs for *what they are* rather than as *who you are.*

LIVING YOUR TRUTH. It is my intention to show you how to re-instate the truth about yourself and your *right-feeling-way-up* will provide you with the completely different starting place to do that. With your new way of looking at old ways of looking at life, you'll experience your first glimpse of life from *all you truly are.* Until today of course, your head was not aware that you could ever make such enlightened discovery about yourself. Your head has only

> Once your heart and your head are in alignment with the truth of who you are, then you will have made lasting change in yourself.

ever learned to store as memory the programming you had learned to give it. Fortunately, your heart can tell the difference between things learned and stored and truths known and felt. That is why your head has much to discover from your heart.

Turning your life the other way around from the way you had been given to understand it, is also how you will transcend your addictive behaviors. It's how to be free. Once your heart and your head are in alignment with the truth of who you are, then you will have made lasting change in yourself.

All of the accumulated thoughts, beliefs, expectations, definitions and behaviors you had amassed about yourself have been sitting in your memory bank of stored data. They are what you hold in your unconscious mind *about* yourself. Notice that they are an accumulation of judgments about yourself, things you've collected along the way. They are judgments you have made into truths about yourself and, until today, you have been living your life by them without even knowing it. No wonder you have never felt good enough. How could it ever have felt good enough to live up to limitations that were made up about your Self?

Your addictive behaviors belong to the meaning you once learned to give to your *upside-down* version of life. They were of course being made from a place of judgment, as indeed everything else about yourself had always been made. Now, from your place of awareness, your addictive behaviors provide the necessary contrast for you to feel your way back into your newly emerging Self. That's how powerful your new discovery is!

Life provides you with contrast so you may navigate your way more easily through it; for without hot, how can you know cold? Without up there is no down. Without left how would you know right? Unless you know who you are not, how can you know who you truly *are*? Using the contrast of your life experiences you can now make the changes you desire, and you'll do that most readily from an awareness of *who you are not*.

You might think of the time you are entering now as your becoming more consciously aware. None of us begin life knowing who we are or why we are the way we are. We have to search deeply to make that discovery. However, once that first stirring of curiosity is triggered, amazing things begin to happen and it is my intention to keep triggering your curiosity about your Self, now that I have your attention. With your curiosity alerted, new ways of looking at old ways of looking at your life begin to happen.

There is no doubt in my mind, that your *addicting* will always have been bound up in your pursuit of your Self. You may have been conscious of that, but in all probability you were not. It's just that the curiosity, which once took you down the path of addiction, is now being re-routed. You've been crying out to the universe: *"There must be more to my life than this!"* And indeed, there is. There is much more to YOU, than you are aware.

BECOMING MORE CONSCIOUSLY AWARE. You are about to see why all the heartache, frustration, confusion and disruption in your life has brought you to this revolution. It has provided you with the contrast necessary to make the discovery you desire. Your addictive behaviors, and your other vulnerabilities, can now act as a kind of backdrop to your next experience of yourself, because no experience is without its purpose.

As you become more *consciously aware* you will begin to remember all you truly are. From that new starting place, it is possible to *transcend* your unwanted behaviors, rather than having to *fight* them. Make no mistake about it ... *transcending* addictive behaviors—by becoming more consciously aware—is how you evolve, how you make change and how to be free. It opens a new way of looking at old ways of looking at life, your life. It's being the "observer" of life, rather than the "do-*er*". From that starting place, everything falls differently into place, for you no longer experience life as if you are separate from it.

JORDAN'S STORY | "The first time I used narcotics I was 11 years old. I had begun hanging around with older kids at school, going to house parties and meeting girls and all the stuff older teenagers were doing. One night, at a house party, I was offered cocaine by a girl I liked. I had never touched drugs before then but wanted to fit in. I took it. It was this moment that changed the entire course of my life.

Prior to ever using drugs, I had felt like I was different. I had always felt alone, unloved. This was, of course, a fallacy and I know that now. In truth, I had a wonderful family of two sisters, a loving mother and a supportive father. But this didn't matter at the time; something just didn't feel right in me.

The very first moment I took a line of cocaine, I felt a sense of belonging I had never felt before. I felt like others loved me, that I had a purpose. I became confident and could talk to people like I had never been able to before. My ego inflated ten times its original size. I had found my cure for my sad state of being. I believe that my brain recorded this moment as my solution to all of life's problems and I used cocaine, marijuana and hallucinogenic substances as my "solutions" for many years to follow.

By the age of seventeen, I recognised that I had an extreme alcohol and cocaine problem. Although I was aware that I could not stop, I did not care. I did not know how to live without these substances and nor did I want to. On my 21st birthday I had a party in a crack house. I went downstairs with my friend to snort some coke and hang out. By this time I was already dealing drugs to pay for my habit and as a result of this I had to carry a fire arm. I had a 22 Browning pistol in my waistband and my friend asked if he could see it. As I handed him the gun, it discharged. The bullet fired through his throat and out of the back of his head. While he lay bleeding on the floor, I found myself taking the drugs out of his pocket. I justified this at the time stating that I didn't want his parents to know he was a drug addict but today I realize I did this because of my addiction and the fact that I simply wanted the dope.

After that night things got really bad. I internalized all my anger and remorse around this situation and started smoking heroin and cocaine mixers to numb the pain. I found myself on multiple occasions in prison for long stay, where I would get clean, only to relapse again when I was released. I didn't want to use anymore but I couldn't stop. My addiction overpowered all other thoughts. My mind was attacking my body and my body was attacking my mind. It was a constant battle.

I began having drug induced seizures and I was barely able to get dope into my body without shutting down. I was going to die. I had a call one day from a friend asking me to meet him at a place he gave me the name and address of. Being high, I automatically presumed it was a bar. I showed up and when I walked in I realized it was a Narcotics Anonymous meeting. I had a single moment of clarity where I realized I could run or I could sit my ass down and listen for the first time. I stayed at that meeting and I listened but, more importantly, I surrendered and accepted that a new path was emerging. I still attend Narcotics Anonymous today.

Shortly after, I was contacted by the RCMP (Canadian Police Force) and entered into the witness protection agency, as I was to testify in a double murder trial against several past friends of mine. Although this was a stressful burden, I also saw it as an opportunity for me to move on. I had been unable to pay my rent or feed myself. I found it difficult to be around others or show love to those in my life. I felt trapped and knew that I had to move away and take the fresh start I was being granted in life, something I never thought would ever be possible. I lost contact with God and it felt very lonely. I could be in the middle of a room filled with people and still feel as though I was alone. I lived a life inside my head. I thought that I was the guy others used as an example, an example of how they didn't want their kids to be like when they grew up.

Several months later I met John Flaherty and my life took on a whole new course of wonder and amazement. John taught me that I was not the same person as I was yesterday. Yesterday was gone and so was that person. John's way of mentoring is like no other. He helped me realize my potential. He opened up a whole new world of possibilities to me and most importantly, John taught me to see how my ego can be beneficial if used in the correct way, but it's not who I am.

I know now that God did for me what I was unable or unwilling to do for myself. I could even say that God directed me every step of the road. I asked my mother for help one time and she told me that I wasn't a drug addict. I believe that she meant well and didn't want me to label myself, but I needed help and this wasn't much of a resolution. Narcotics Anonymous had accepted me with open arms and John showed me love, kindness and compassion. He accepted me without judgment and so did other recovering addicts. We can often understand each other without bias.

Harm reduction didn't work for me. Unless I practiced total abstinence I would always find myself back using in no time. Every time this happened it got worse.

Death and loss always made the problem worse. I never knew how to cope with that. It wasn't so much the death and loss in itself but the fact that I didn't know how to experience emotions of grief or sadness, without using drugs or alcohol to numb it out.

John was the first person to ever tell me I was capable of anything. He gave me permission to change everything about myself. There are no restrictions in life. Now I know that if I allow God (Source) to move through me it becomes a partnership. I can do whatever I desire to do in life. There are things I used to do that I don't need anymore and there are things now that I never thought I could do. I am not who I was yesterday. I am not even Jordan. I am part of Source and therefore able to harness all the power in the universe if I am willing to do so.

John taught action. He showed me how to meditate. He taught me mantras to use during the day and to actually try on these new life skills instead of just talking about them. The meditation training enabled me to self reflect without the need for outside influences. He showed me how to use energy tapping on my body to bring calm and most important of all, John showed me how to understand forgiveness.

Forgiveness isn't about making the other person feel better, it is about me letting go and not allowing others to hurt me anymore inside my heart and my head. Resentments used to feel like they weighed a thousand pounds and when I had lots, it was hard to move through life carrying all that weight. Letting go and forgiving others allowed me to dump that weight and simply put, I began to feel weightless. I learned that acceptance was simply self forgiveness which is just as important as forgiving others. Yesterday is done and I can't go back to change things. I can only focus on today and how I use it.

My life has now changed 180 Degrees. My perception of the world and those around me was of takers. Everyone and everything only wanted to take from me but today I see the world and those in it as a place of rebirth and opportunity.

I received just as much peace from letting go as I did from the knowledge that I am capable of letting go. I forgave myself for the death of my friend. I forgave myself for the atrocities of my past life and I forgave others for not interceding when I needed help the most. Today I take responsibility for my own life and if others wish to positively contribute to it, I let them do so.

I know now that my ego stood in the way of me listening to others. Once I discovered that, I learned to listen to other people's experiences. I now encourage other's on their own journey. I make every moment a teachable moment now that I understand myself as an infinite being, capable of love and forgiveness and acceptance. I choose today to not identify myself as anything else. I have become an Addiction Counselor, assisting other people with everything that assisted me. I have a wonderful partner in my life today as well as her five year old child that I love as my own. This is the first and only relationship I have ever had that was healthy, responsive to change and honest.

I have regained trust, love and respect from my friends and family. I have money in my bank account and people in my life have respect for me. I have manageable feelings, thoughts and emotions. I'm able to cry and I'm no longer ashamed to do so. I've learned what love really is. I have given myself permission to remove all fears and limitations in my day to day and my future. I spend my days in service to others and to myself. Most importantly, I have been free of all drugs and alcohol for almost four years. I am free of mental obsessions and an agitated state of mind and body. Spirituality has made sense of life.

I have learned from mistakes and I use them to change my behaviors. I had to let go of some friends in my life as they were negative people. Correction, I didn't have to let them go. I chose to let them go. I always find new things to implement. I read stories of great people in the history of the world and do as they did. Most have one thing in common. They all lived a life free of fear. I have learned to do the same.

I'm kinesthetic, so I learn best with hands on experience and I need to repeat things long enough till they take. Some new things take longer than others but I live a life of progress not perfection. John has shown me how to direct my day, instead of letting things direct or upset me. Every morning I get to choose how my day goes. If I wake up and go straight into a problem, I stop and pull out from it. It's like I'd just stubbed my toe. It reminds me to just lay back down and reset my mind before leaving the house. Then I don't spend the whole day feeling like I'm repeatedly stubbing my toe! I have a purpose today, to be purposeful in my actions. Today I love life. I used to dread waking up in the morning because I never knew what turmoil I had caused the night before. Now I wake up ready to take on all of life's twists and turns.

"Don't forget to remember." These words of John remind me of where I came from and where I am today. They encourage me to continuously change my stars. Life is not set in stone. I didn't just draw the short straw. I can be whoever I want to be, whenever I choose to be it, because I am the one who is now aware of what I'm choosing."

CHAPTER THREE

When you woke up this morning, how did you know to be you?

If you are pained by external things, it is not that they disturb you, but your own judgment of them. And it is in your own power to wipe out that judgment now.

—Marcus Aurelius

As you opened your eyes this morning and, even before you pushed back the blankets to begin a new day, how did you know to be you? In other words, how did you know what belief to believe about you, what thought to begin your day thinking, what behavior you should start behaving? After all, it was a brand new day with nothing set in stone about it or about you. Your only cue, was where you left off before going to sleep the night before. True? That's how you knew to be you. You continued on into auto-pilot mode from where you left off last night. Your first thought connected to your last one, your first belief continued on from your last one, your behavior was simply a copy-cat action of your previous repetitive ones. You knew how to be you, by unquestioningly living out the programmed ways by which you have been conditioned.

ADDICTION OR INSANITY? Addiction is to keep on doing what you have always done before, desperately expecting difference and feeling like you just can't stop. It was Albert Einstein who said, *"Insanity is doing the same thing over and over again and expecting different results."*

So what society calls addiction, Einstein describes as insanity. Are they one and the same? You may or may not think so, but there is no mistaking the similarity of their matching pattern and characteristics. It is an important thing to ask questions like this. If nothing else, the answers will give the clue as to how mainstream addiction programs are basing their own recovery processes. Are they primarily about correcting behaviors, turning a *bad* behavior into a *good* one, an *unacceptable* one into an *acceptable* one? If they are, is it ever possible to know when the job is done? What does the finished product look like? What behavior is now being behaved and who is it that's going to be most satisfied with the end result? What does *good* look like?

In my experience of working with those in private residential rehab treatment centers, it was always interesting to observe who the *good* or the *bad* outcome was most often being judged by.

Inevitably, once admitted into rehab and having spent an initial period of their stay detoxifying, each resident would quickly begin to relax and feel more at ease in their new found environment. They felt safe once they were out of their own regular routines, where drug or alcohol intake had become so much part of their day to day repetitious behavior. Companionship would strike up with peers, better eating habits would be enjoyed, sleep would be improved, exercise be taken and a natural joy would again arise. Then, the greatest test of all would come, and it was always in the unsuspecting form of family weekend!

FEAR OF NON-ACCEPTANCE. No matter how far advanced each person was in their rehabilitation time, a sudden fear and dread would fill each resident at the prospect of a visit from or a return to their families. Why was that so? From my observation the answer became crystal clear. The residents had taken the necessary *time-out* to reflect and contemplate on who they'd learned to become. They had discovered who they were NOT and were beginning to uncover who they more truly were. Only one major hurdle stood in their way, and it was the fear of non-acceptance by those nearest and dearest to them.

MAKING RIGHT A WRONG? Mainstream addiction recovery programs place enormous emphasis on the need for recovering addicts to make amends with family and to be repentant for all wrong-doing. For most, such an obligation was often too big a step to take. Such an expectation does little to remove judgment, for it keeps in place the belief that

> Addiction is never about one person not knowing how to do life the right way. There is no right or wrong way, only someone else's preference for it to be as they judge it.

the only person to have been in error is the addict. The onerous responsibility not to *mess up* again or bare the consequences, is the commitment each person entering recovery feels resigned to undertake. Such expectations are arrogant to say the least and are rarely possible or even necessary to fulfill. They are a missed opportunity for others to similarly grasp life's invitation to make their own discoveries for self-growth at the same time. Addiction is never about one person not knowing how to *do* life the *right* way. There is no *right* or *wrong* way, only someone else's preference for it to be as they judge it. The addiction people are most prone to is the necessity to be *right* about things, as you may have discovered.

In most cases of course, families pay a lot of money for their spouse or their son or daughter to go to rehab and to be made *right*. They don't expect their own life-changes to be part of the remit. Their value for money is mistakenly assessed by whether the addict returns to them *"fixed"*. The expectation being that once their loved one was fixed, they'd be normal again, more like themselves! That would be *good*. The inference here is that once the addict is more like their family members, they will be acceptable again, possibly even lovable again. For many of those in addiction, that was not going to be an expectation they could ever guarantee living up to. They knew too well that it was this same expectation that was at the very cause of their addictions in the first place.

TRANSCENDING JUDGMENT, FEAR AND ADDICTION. Once an individual becomes more consciously aware and discovers more of their true nature, the last thing required from anyone else is approval or disapproval. The process of Self-discovery, Self-awareness and Self-empowerment does not depend

> **Just as the process of birth and death can only be for you to go through, so it is with your decision to move beyond your addictions.**

on the judgment of another person. Transcending your addictions does not rely on your ability to fulfill the requests of another. As you move beyond your addictions, life is simultaneously giving your family and those close to you, the same invitation to transcend their own judgments and limitations. They too are being invited to expand in the conscious awareness of everything that they'd previously missed about life before now. Be careful not to try saving another person from receiving the same gift as you are being offered. Life is simply making the same gift to them as it's making to you and for the same purpose, albeit through different circumstances. That's how powerful life's invitation is and you not getting in the way of its message, is another measure of how powerful you are!

Transcending addictions is the process of giving yourself back to your Self and it's a matter only you can decide. Just as the process of birth and death can only be for you to go through, so it is with your decision to move beyond your addictions.

Now, there is so very much more in that wonderful process of change that is missed by mainstream recovery programs. It's really what the process of *transcending* addictions, rather than working to *beat* or *overcome* them, can ultimately bring to everyone involved. Too much emphasis is placed on the addict being the only person life is inviting to change. Life does not work that way, for life does not judge.

LIFE'S INVITATION. The invitation that life is making to all of us, all of the time, is to constantly evolve, constantly change, constantly grow and create ourselves anew. That's the nature of all creation and it's never just about you.

As you create your various creations, some of them will inevitably appear as challenges to others. Your addictive behaviors have been a challenge to yourself, but also to others, for no challenge affects only one individual. Your challenges, however, are also invitations and that is as applicable to others, as it is to yourself. When you are transcending your addictions, just as it is when you are lost in them, your decisions simultaneously affect the lives of others. That which is perceived as challenge, is really only life's *invitation*. Life is inviting *everyone* who has been affected an opportunity to discover more about who they are. In this instance, ironically enough, life's invitation for others to grow is actually coming about through the creation of your addictive behavior. That is just how life works. The challenge and invitation being thrown up to others by your behaviors, extends the same opportunity to them as your addictions have created for you; that each may evolve, change, grow and be created anew.

Just as no one could prevent the experience you have been having through your addictions, you cannot be the one to deprive another of the opportunity life is inviting them to encounter. Life will provide its invitation as uniquely to others as it has to yourself. There is no necessity for you to fear how others will manage or cope with the challenges that they are encountering. Trying to save another from their own individual challenges, is trying to live another person's life for them. It's just not possible.

SELF AND MUTUAL RESPECT. If your family are able to accept you as you are, they go free. If you are able to accept yourself as you are, you go free. Once expectations and conditions are made on another to conform in order to be accepted, suffering is the only outcome. Just as your addictions have been life's invitation to you to move through them and into the grander experience of yourself, the chaos for those nearest to you is no less their opportunity to move through their own challenges. They will manage or not, just as well as you will, or not. Trying to keep a relationship intact that's based on the fear of another person's possible rejection of you, however, is no longer an option.

If your family are able to accept you as you are, they go free. If you are able to accept yourself as you are, you go free.

As you become more consciously aware, you naturally begin to relate to all others from a place of self and mutual respect. When there's mutual

respect, you allow all other's to be that which they are. There's no requirement of you to change another person. There's no requirement to conform
to another's demands of you. You do not require others to be anything or
in any way different to how they are being. You don't need to try accom-
modating their behavior, just as other's don't need to accommodate yours.
Allowing is all that is necessary. Then there's no judgment involved, and
without judgment, each person goes free.

The expansion of your conscious awareness is not dependent on
others being able to expand with you. As you expand, life invites others
to do likewise. They can grab the opportunity or let it pass by unnoticed.
You have let many opportunities pass by before this time and now you
have taken notice. Only in the absence of fear can compassionate love
and acceptance from another and for another be made possible. For as
long as that essential discovery about life is missed, everything about life's
invitation is missed. The difference for you this time around is that you're
more consciously aware that you can no longer afford to miss another of
life's invitations. That would be the insanity Einstein refers to, of doing
the same thing over and over again and expecting different results. Having
discovered enough from your addictive behaviors, it is now totally optional
whether or not to choose insanity over freedom.

NEGATIVE EMOTIONAL TIES. The emotional bond to your family ties are
understandably the most difficult from which to cut the ties. Yet, when
those ties are negative and are stifling your growth, it's crucial to free them.
Emotional pain results from negative relationships and experiences and
registers in your body as acutely as physical pain. Emotional pain cannot
be treated effectively with morphine, anesthetics or addictions. You may
well have tried some, if not all, of those attempts in the past. Addictions
simply numb your emotional pain, they don't address it and they certainly
don't heal it.

When it comes to pain, the only way out is through. You have to feel
it to heal it. When you popped out from your mother's womb, you were able
to express pain, through breathing, crying and moving. As time has gone

on, you've forgotten to re-member your natural power to do this. Instead, you have learned to replace it by suppressing your natural processes. You have done so, simply because you were taught that to acknowledge and express your pain would be viewed by others as a sign of weakness. Now that you are ready to give yourself back to your Self, this is yet another of your learned behaviors to be aware of. It has not been serving you or others well and it's time to unlearn it, fast.

If you feel like crying, cry. If you have learned to substitute physical fitness to avoid feeling, then sit still with your pain and feel it to intensity until it is done. Or, if you avoid movement, avoid interaction with other things and other people in order to avoid pain, get moving again. Feel the pain and release it as you go. Your addiction is a suppression, it is masking deep emotional pain, pain not yet acknowledged. Begin your discovery process by first acknowledging that, then give yourself permission to be in pain and the permission to free it. You have been suppressing many things and trying to live all that you are NOT. It is time to step out from your box. Time to be free.

Addiction is the profound absence of natural joy. When you feel what is naturally within you to express, know that it is your heart reminding you to be true to your feeling. When you resist the prompting to release your natural expression and instead keep yourself suppressed, be aware that it is your head rather than your heart calling the shots. Know that your head cannot heal pain. Only your heart can do that. Your head will only give you an unlimited number of justifications for holding on to it, for that is the way its been programmed to react. The essential joy that is at the center of your Being will return to the surface as you express your feelings naturally once again. Then pain is released and you begin once more to feel the connectivity with your Source. You emerge stronger and return yourself to your Self. All feels well again.

Understand that all pain is made far worse when you keep yourself apart from your own heart and judge yourself in any way. I will repeat that, because your addiction is the behavior resulting from the life-time you have spent doing this very thing ...

Understand that all pain is made far worse when you keep yourself apart from your own heart and judge yourself in any way.

If you have grown up with a sense of incompleteness from your childhood, but haven't known quite what that incompleteness was, then the explanation I have just given you will make sense. If you have longed for but haven't received acceptance from your parents, your mother in particular, from whose body you were birthed, then this explanation will make sense. If you have had loving parents and have often said, *"I know my parents loved me, but ..."* then this explanation will make sense. If you have wanted to be reconciled with your parents and craved their unconditional love, then this explanation will make sense to you. If you have felt your parents haven't understood you well enough, then this explanation will make sense to you. If you have had a traumatic childhood and experienced abuse in any of its many forms, then this explanation will make sense. If you have no recollection at all of your childhood, but never felt like you have ever been able to *fit-in* to life or be easy in the company of other people, this explanation will make sense to you.

What you are feeling in your sense of incompleteness will have inevitably shown up in your life as one of these experiences. It is, however, about so much more than that experience alone. It is ultimately down to the fact that you have been desiring from your parents that which only your Source can adequately provide. There is space between you and your parents and necessarily so, but you are not and never can you be separate from the Source of life that is sourcing you.

The sense of incompleteness you feel is because the fusion between you and your parents is not as bonded as it is between you and the Source of life, from which all life is sourced. It is not meant to feel the same, but you have become conditioned to believe it is the same, and there lies

Your mother and father are your parents, parenting you. They are not the Source, sourcing you.

your confusion. In times when life has been challenging, you have been seeking acceptance and approval from those through whom you were birthed. When it hasn't been able to come freely to you from them, and in the sufficiency you have craved, you have felt separated from life itself. Your mother and father are your parents, parenting you. They are not your Source, sourcing you. Become conscious of this truth, your conscious awareness changes everything. Love your parents and receive love from them, but know your life's not lived for them or by them.

HEALING PAINFUL MEMORIES. All problems begin with a thought, but having a thought is not the problem. The problem is that all thoughts are imbued with painful memories of people, places or things. Many of them of course, stem from your early childhood and have continued to play out in your life ever since. Your head will try managing the problems that have brought pain, but managing problems is not what you want. You want to let them go!

Try this experiment:

The process I am about to introduce to you is essentially about freedom, complete freedom from your past. Become aware of your breathing and be very much aware that you are the individual expression of consciousness, the microcosm of the macrocosm of Infinite Consciousness. It's how you have been experiencing the Self of you in the human form that you have come to THINK of as you.

No matter what has happened in your life-time that is still causing you deep pain, thank yourself for your willingness to bring your time and attention to it. Acknowledge your pain and, once you do, allow yourself to feel it no matter how uncomfortable it is. Literally sit with the discomfort of it until it no longer holds dominion over you. You can bring more lightness into your life again, but not without acknowledging the darkness of confusion your painful memories hold for you. Your pain has gifted you the opportunity to do something about it and now you can ...

Go within and say: *"Thank You"* and keep repeating your thanks. The way to move out of judgment is to move into gratitude. When you bring an end to judgment, you bring an end to pain. Deeply express your heartfelt gratitude for your new discovery. When you bring an end to pain, you bring an end to an entire way of living. Your expression of gratitude is in recognition that your pain is real and your desire to free yourself of it is now equally real and intent. This is no small thing. This is a life-changing shift in attitude and behavior. It's the miracle you're about to discover you can perform. That's how powerful you are!

In recalling the negative memories associated with your pain, they will become present in your awareness. Just become aware of them. Judgment is not required. As they arrive, begin to neutralize the energy associated with the memory or the confusion that's evoked such pain in you. You allow this by visualizing yourself purifying the energy that has been spent over the years accumulating as your pain. Continue doing so, by simply repeating the words *"Thank You"*. The process will be complete when it feels complete to you.

By neutralizing your painful memories, you return yourself to your natural place of personal peace and harmony. Your memories have their existence in the past and the past is now passed. You are living in the now, where neither past nor future can possibly reside. Your *"Thank You"* is your acknowledgment of that realization. FEEL the restoration your realization brings. All is well. Keep expressing *"Thank You"* for the freedom of this realization.

Next voice the words to yourself:
"I'm sorry, please forgive me"

You need to release the negative energy that keeps you from moving forward. To forgive isn't to condone another person's abusive or destructive behavior. Forgiveness is accepting that behavior without judgment and then releasing it into the light. Your forgiveness is not directed at any specific person or any one thing, only yourself. Forgive yourself for forgetting to re-member who you truly are. You had mistaken your made-up self, the ego, for your true Self. Only in doing so, was it possible for you to have held such pain without releasing it before today. The Hebrew word for *forgiveness* translates to *drop it*, and that is what you need to do: Release a hurt from the past or a person who has hurt you so that you can make your life whole.

You have been trying to remedy painful memories, by blocking them or by trying to manage them intellectually, but managing things is not the way to solve problems. Dissolve them and let them go! Now, the present, is the time to do that. In the now is the only place you can ever be, and in the now problems do not exist. Only by filling your present with an imagined future, built on a negative memory of the past, has it been possible to have kept feeling pain in the now. Forgive yourself for your forgetfulness of that truth. That's how powerful you are!

Finally, keep voicing the words: *"I Love You"* and return yourself to your Self as you do so. Love is how to heal. Take time to feel love sweeping across your mind and your body, let it take up its more natural presence in you. Once it has, savor the immediate freedom and well-being it brings. Love yourself back into life.

The healing process described above comes from the practice of the ancient Hawaiian civilization. The powerful problem-solving system is known as Ho'oponopono.

HO' OPONOPONO | The wonderful thing about Ho'oponopono is that it takes people out of the intellect and ego and back to their true nature. You don't really have to know what the specific problem is that you are addressing. All you have to become aware of is the fact that if it's still causing you physical, mental or emotional pain, it's still there! Once aware of the pain, it's within your power and it's your responsibility to immediately clear it and go free. Making judgment of another person for the cause of your pain is unnecessary. If it's a pain that has come about from your past and is still remaining in your awareness, then no matter who was at fault, only you can have the ability to free yourself of it. Take 100% responsibility for your freedom. Recognize that if pain from the past is still in your present, then you are still attracting it to you, for like attracts like.

Ho'oponopono means to make right.

*As you set yourself free, others who you
identify as being part of your pain, are also set free.*

That's how powerful you are!

Repeat this process of *Ho'oponopono* as often as is needed. Releasing pain is not a one-off event, it's part of your life experience as a human being to regularly encounter pain. As you use the process, you release endorphins and encourage a "shift" to take place in your emotional system, so that pain is naturally and immediately released. This I suggest, is how to better understand what is most often referred to as the need for forgiveness, or the need for "letting go". This is the most thorough and complete way I've discovered to release pain and to remain free. I've been privileged to share *Ho'oponopono* with very many people who were also ready to be free. Now you are amongst them.

CHAPTER FOUR

Conscious awareness

What lies behind us and what lies before us are
tiny matters, compared to what lies within us.

–Ralph Waldo Emerson

Conscious awareness, becoming the observer of yourself and of all that is within your energy field, enables you to move beyond each and every one of your experiences. Significantly, it also prevents past emotional or mental pain remaining as an experience of suffering in your present. Pain is inevitable in life, but suffering is totally optional. When you discover how to literally *watch* the things that are happening and watch the things that you are "doing", rather than getting caught up in them or being the victim of them, you go free. There is never a need to judge the actions you are observing. Judgment keeps pain in place. Just watch, discover and, when necessary, take the action appropriated from your conscious awareness.

YOUR POWERFUL OBSERVER SELF. As you make the radical change of observing life while it's playing out, a totally new you is brought into existence. Life has already equipped you with enough experiences, along with the contrast necessary, to expand your vision of yourself. By being closely aware of everything, you are observing a new dimension of yourself. Like sun-light dispersing early morning mist, your conscious awareness is sufficient to remove you out from all your programming. You begin to see that you are not the thoughts about yourself that are running through your head, you're the one who is now *aware* that there are thoughts passing through your head. Each thought you have is completely random, as you will observe. Each is disconnected from the other, as you will observe. Only the consciously unaware person does not realize this. Once that changes in you, everything changes for you. So begin watching. Watch every desire that takes possession of you. Watch every act you do. Before today, you had not known how to make the distinction between your random passing thoughts and your Self. Now you do. As you become aware of that power, savor another new discovery about your Self.

Savor this newly emerging realization too ...

If you are not the thought that you are currently thinking, but the one who is now able to observe yourself *having* thoughts, who is the YOU that's doing the observing? One thing is for sure, you are not confined to the physical body you have been believing yourself to be.

As soon as you become aware of your expanded consciousness and as you get more practiced at experiencing it, the Self of you becomes less difficult for you to comprehend. At the same time, the ego-self, you had learned to become, begins to feel less significant, less important. You can now determine your behavior and your decision making, rather than letting your learned version of yourself determine and define you.

As you feel how freeing it is to know you can choose your next thought before you have it, know too that when it feels useful to think it, you can save it. When a thought feels disempowering to you, you can delete it. After all, it's only a thought, you don't ever have to believe a thought. The average person will have an estimated 65,000-90,000 thoughts per day. That's a huge number of thoughts to be bombarded by isn't it? What's even more disconcerting is that 90% of those random thoughts are the ones you had yesterday! From your place of awareness, you can now select which of those thoughts, if any, you would like to give attention to and which ones you can just let pass. To get a first sense of how much more than your thoughts YOU are, see how difficult it is to have your next thought, once you've become conscious of it. Go ahead right now and try. Try hard, try really hard to have your very next thought and, now that you're observing it, you'll discover that it just won't come. That's how powerful you are!

Conscious awareness also removes the need to rate your life experiences or the thoughts that accompany them as either *good* or *bad*, *right* or *wrong*. Rating your life experiences is an endless task, always requiring judgment of yourself, judgment of another and judgment about life. Judgment is the behavior you learned from an early age. It's the behavior that keeps every one of your unwanted *stories* and behaviors intact and unchanged. A judgment of another need not concern you either, for worrying how you may have been judged also keeps things unwanted as things unchanged. Other people's judgments say more about their own "story" than they say about yours.

> Rating your life experiences is an endless task, always requiring judgment of yourself, judgment of another and judgment about life.

From your place of awareness you can observe the way your body reacts to a certain thought or a certain emotion, without needing to judge it and without the necessity of letting it dominate your physical and mental state. In other words, you can observe an emotion arising in you and, as soon as you sense its arrival, you can either choose to *feel* it into being, or you can just let it pass. In watching your emotions, you can remain detached from them, just as you can when you watch your passing thoughts. Judgment energizes thoughts and emotions. Only judgment makes them real. Without judgment they affect nothing.

It is interesting to observe that it is judgment that makes the difference between a workaholic and an alcoholic. Workaholics think they are doing *right* and generally speaking, their learned behavior is often regarded as being perfectly acceptable. Alcoholics think they are doing *wrong* and generally speaking, their behavior is not tolerated and regarded as totally unacceptable. In truth, both the workaholic behavior and the alcoholic behavior are falsehoods driven by your made up version of yourself, the ego. Both hold a belief in lack. The workaholic judges that there may not be enough time. The alcoholic judges there may not be enough to satisfy their craving. What each has in common is the belief that such a requirement exists; that need exists, that insufficiency exists and most significantly that failure exists.

NO-THING IN LIFE IS FAILURE. The notion of failure is a judgment and without judgment, you will always feel so much more *in tune* with the movement of life itself. Only judgment causes suffering and, as you are now aware, while pain is inevitable in life, suffering is always totally optional.

When you are free of judgment you remain free of suffering. Know too, that as you go through life, you will experience a whole range of different emotions, but there are only two feelings; those that feel in tune and those that feel out of tune. Emotions are not the same as feelings. As you observe an emotion welling up inside that makes you feel in tune, save it. If there is an emotion that brings negativity and does not make you feel in tune, delete it. Your head cannot choose to do this, it has not yet learned how. To make your next discovery, you must enter the realm that goes beyond thoughts and emotions, beyond what you can see and can think. Your heart will show you the way. As you become aware of a feeling within you, even if it remains unidentifiable but which brings a peaceful, sometimes joyous, freeing connectivity, know you are in tune with life itself, that which is sourcing you.

AWARENESS IS EVERYTHING. As you become more consciously aware, not only can you begin to understand how your life has been the experience it has been, you can also clearly see how to take responsibility for it. Judgment is the first thing for you to dissolve. It has not been serving you well. Not only has it obscured from your awareness the power of your own true potential, it has created the mistaken belief that you can be separate from your Source.

As the *Being* observing your life, rather than the *Do-er* judging your life, take a bird's eye view of it all now. With your new way of looking at old ways of looking at life, just see what you have been missing and discover all that there is to be newly

> Judgment is the first thing for you to dissolve. It has not been serving you well.

experienced ...

Try this experiment:

Close your eyes and turn within. Do it right now for several minutes or for as long as possible before your chattering self-talk breaks in, like the ill mannered gate-crasher it has got used to being. You will find yourself in a blackness, a darkness, but the very place where that darkness is, is your means of access to Infinity, to your Being, to the pure potential that you *are*. In your acknowledgment of this, you are ready for new truths to emerge about your Self. New truths do not come from without, they come from within. They do not come from anyone else to you, they are realizations that come from the Self of you to you. They come from the center to the circumference of you, from the depths of your Being to the surface of your Being. You bring about new truths by turning within and realizing the power of consciousness. Through consciousness, you have access to depths of your Being that were not as apparent or as accessible to you before.

When you are so busy *doing* life, so caught up in every thought, every drama, every action and every re-action, you lose all sense of your Self. Your head dominates with the accumulation of *things* about yourself that you have collected along the way: judgments that you have mistakenly made into truths about your life. Your mind becomes a disturbance of consciousness, much as waves are a disturbance of the ocean and there is chaos. Yet the chaos is always on the surface. The waves are always on the surface. There are no waves in the depths of the ocean, because in the depths, disturbance cannot enter. There is no wind to create waves and to disturb the depths. In the same way, if you move inward from the surface of yourself to your center, *you* are not disturbed. This is why meditation is so vital. Meditation is nothing but centering, moving towards your center, getting rooted there. From your center, the whole perspective of life changes. The waves may still be there, but they don't reach you. You can watch the waves. You might even enjoy observing them, but they no longer threaten, they no longer engulf you, they no longer dominate. Similarly, even when you are not in meditation, continue to be the observer of your life. Watch every act that you do, even small gestures—walking, talking, eating, taking a bath. Let everything be an opportunity to watch.

WHEN YOU WATCH, A CLARITY ARISES. The more you watch and observe without judgment, the more your chattering self-talk chatters less. The more you watch, all your hastiness slows down. That is because the energy you once used for negative self-talk you are now consciously using for watchfulness. It is the same energy, put to a greater expansion of yourself than to the depletion of yourself. The more and more energy used for watchfulness, the less is given to the thoughts and emotions that are burdensome.

If you eat watchfully, food will become more tasty. Eat slowly, chew and taste each bite. Similarly, as you go about other actions, smell, touch, feel every detail. You will be surprised at how much you have been missing and how much satisfaction you have gone without. With practice, the more watchful you become, the less persistent your negative self-talk will be. That nagging, negative and judgmental self-talk is your head trying to constantly feed you with the programming it has been fed over the years. Your head chatter doesn't like being monitored and it doesn't take kindly to being interrupted. It's got very used to being in charge and you have been unwittingly giving it such authority. Now you have just made your next freeing discovery. This is how to unplug the very energy supply you had been giving to your addictive behaviors. You now reclaim the charge given to your life in a very different way.

As you become the observer of your actions, the observer of your thoughts, the observer of your negative self-talk and the observer of your feelings, you discover how to be free. By being the observer of your life, you become more consciously aware that you not only have a new way of looking at your old ways of looking at life, you now know there is so much more to YOU than you had been aware of before!

SEE HOW GOOD IT FEELS TO BE YOU. By expanding your conscious awareness, you can perceive the *all* of life. No longer limited by the learned behavior that has been conditioning everything that goes on *inside* of you,

you now open the possibilities of how to change your perception of the *outside* world as well. As the observer, you can do and see things you never knew you could do or see before. Even time is differently affected. In your more consciously aware state, you will observe how time moves much slower. Your life goes at a slower pace where you have the ability to watch and then choose, instead of living life hurriedly reacting and then regretting.

Your Zen-like practice of being always present in the moment, rather than being swept away by the external activities of the day, changes how you perceive *everything*. How you think about things, how you feel about things and how you sense the world is now experienced by who you are, rather than by who you had learned to become. Things will at last be observed from your more *right-feeling-way-up* and no longer from the *upside-down* version of the life you learned to live out.

Without constant head chatter running your life, you will get your first crystal clear experience of your Self. You are NOT the thoughts and you are NOT the emotions running through your head. You are the observer of your life. Watch and observe how you have been living it and decide how you now prefer to experience it. That's how powerful you are!

BEFORE YOU CAME INTO THE WORLD. Now roll back time and from the place of observer, see what you have been unable to see from the beginning ...

Before you came into the world, you were pure potential, Infinite Consciousness. As soon as you popped out from your mother's womb, that's when the things called "problems" in your individual consciousness first came into being.

You know from your earlier experiment that you are not and never can you be separate from life itself. You have also distinguished between yourself who has become saturated in thoughts and emotions and, the Self of you who is now able to observe yourself *having* thoughts and emotions. You have discovered too that for as long as you *fight* to overcome your problems they remain real. Yet, when you simply allow yourself to observe problems from

As long as you are breathing this moment, then you are clearly still connected to your Source, the Source of life itself.

your center, moving with them, not against them, they disappear. So who are YOU? Who is this newly discovered observer Self that can affect your life-actions and decide differently how to experience them? Who is this YOU that can decide your behaviors rather than have your learned behaviors deciding for you?

As long as you are breathing this moment, then you are clearly still connected to your Source, the Source of life itself. However obvious that may sound, it has not been the starting place from which you readily remembered to approach life when challenges arose. Until today, it hasn't been the starting place you were even aware was available to you. Now it is. That's how powerful you are!

You had largely come to think of yourself as a separate individual; thinking, behaving and acting in your own right, unaware of your shared commonality with other life forms. You had become oblivious to the connectivity you have to a Life Source, yet you know how impossible it is to function otherwise. Without heartbeat, pulse or breath there is no YOU to be you! Put another way, you are not a human *doing*, operating independently from your Source, you are a human *being* and your be-ing requires connectivity in order for you to be present! Now let me cut to the chase about your addictions and put it to you even more starkly ...

Before you received the life-changing message I am delivering to you at this time, you may not have felt equipped to make any lasting change to your addictive behaviors. Perhaps you had not brought into your awareness the deceptive functioning of the ego. Once you make the distinction between your Self and your learned ego-self, a whole new world of possibilities opens up to you. Making the distinction between your true Self and the ego's version of you is the key to an entirely different understanding, not only of your addictions, but of your life: your past, your present and your future.

Let me explain ...

You were born, as every new life-form is birthed, ignited from the Source of life which sources everything. In the nine months you spent in the womb and during the process of birth itself, you were consistently supplied and provided for by the one same Life Source. Yes, I know you have come to believe your parents when they said you were theirs and that they created you, but strictly speaking that is not so, is it? It's more precise to say, that in the action of your parent's sexual union with one another, life created you. You were sourced into being *through* them rather than by them. Until you were ready to be popped out from your mother's womb, you didn't even know your parents, they hadn't yet formed you in their own preferred mould. As far as you were concerned, they certainly hadn't been your Life Source before this time.

> **Making the distinction between your true Self and the ego's version of you, is the key to an entirely different understanding, not only of your addictions but of your life; your past, your present and your future.**

So what happened next? Well, in a nutshell, that is when things called *problems* became known to you. You took one look at your mother, in whose womb you had been incubated and you were told, *"This is your mother ..."* and you took one look at your father, if he was in attendance, and you were told, *"This is your father ..."* Wow! Talk about early chilhood trauma and confusion over identity. Let's face it, no matter how loving your parents are, they don't look like the all-providing, non-demanding, all-nurturing safe Creator you have been sourced by. They don't resonate with quite the same consistency as your Life Source. The constancy of provision you have been receiving from your Source may suddenly seem less dependable, now that you are entrusted to the care of your parents. But who were you to question that? In all circumstances, your parents seem adamant that you are theirs and so you, being new to all of this, step out in trust and accept their ownership.

THE EGO IDENTITY YOU FORMED. From here on in you began to form an identity about yourself, contrived though it was. You were told how much you look and act like various members of your family; in many cases, people you don't even know. You learn that you have your *"mother's eyes"* and you are told you have your *"father's nose"*, you learn how things are going to be, even though they haven't happened yet ... *"You'll be a great sportsman, just like your uncle!"* and, *"You are another stubborn little thing, just like your older brother."* All the time, you were beginning to piece together an image and an identification of yourself as you were taught to live it. This is the ego. It is the learned version of YOU and who you have been living ever since. You were given a name which, not surprisingly, you didn't get to choose for yourself either. You were programmed, conditioned, cloned and named.

As I was fashioned, I became John. Nothing out of the ordinary there. My father was already named John and so was his. I became a Catholic in a matter of weeks. I soon wore the red and white striped colors of the soccer team my family had always supported. It was tradition. Now I was an addition to tradition. From an early stage I was quickly introduced to the family mantra, *"This is how we do things in this family."* And, in the twinkling of an eye, my identity, made up as it was, became cemented. This was now my egoic sense of self and I bought it hook, line and sinker. Well you do don't you? Being the new kid, who hasn't yet learned to speak the lingo.

Now there's nothing unique about my birth process. Your induction was much the same, with you inheriting your own cultural, religious or societal identity as you went along. Not only that, but you inherited borrowed attitudes, borrowed beliefs, borrowed thoughts, borrowed image, borrowed expectations, borrowed fears, borrowed anxieties, borrowed behaviors and borrowed words. All became a life you borrowed, without you even being aware of it. The more you borrowed, the more you forgot to remember your Self. And, so originated the process of you developing who you really are NOT!

The interesting thing, which you will now be able to observe, is that when you wear a *borrowed* mask for so long, you forget who you truly are beneath it. Your addictive behaviors are indicators that you have forgotten to re-member the truth of who you are. They are indicators also of your relentless, though often frustrating, endeavors to reclaim your true expression and purpose in life. It is possible you can spend a life-time trying to overcome that frustration and, indeed, many do. Or, you can dedicate the rest of your days in *recovery* from the fallout of your frustration but progress no further and, indeed, many do. Or, you can just "slip out" from your learned version of yourself and, indeed, many do. I am showing you the way to *slip out* from that learned version of yourself so that you may go free.

DORIAN'S STORY

"I felt completely lost. I didn't know what to do. I knew I needed help but I was simply not able to say, "I need help." A mental war ensued for many years where I'd tell myself that I did not need help and that there was nothing wrong with me. However, that was soon followed by a deluge of negative self-talk. I used to constantly judge myself and the judgment was always negative ... "I'm a loser ... I'm worthless ... I've done nothing with my life." The only reason I ever did end up seeking help was because I discovered that those I loved already knew I had a problem. It wasn't necessary for me to explain myself to people after all. My mental torment and my addictive behaviors had become apparent to those who knew me. There was no use hiding it, it was written all over my face and apparent in all of my actions. I had been a vibrant person who was now living in a self-imposed darkness and I felt very alone.

With the help of family, off I went to a treatment centre. All was going to be well with the world. I would come out "cured." Ha! Now, that was probably the biggest lie ever told. There's no magic "fix" to right a ship that's so wayward it's in the pitch dark. I knew I had to do more than improve a behavior. I had to let it go, totally let it go. Years followed. There were slips and relapses. Nothing seemed to work and little ever changed. I had tried everything imaginable to rid myself of the scourge of addiction. Counseling, treatment centers, psychiatry. You name it, I tried it. My family supported me throughout every attempt, but I was continually left at a loss. Everything still seemed so complicated, so frightening. It wasn't until I met John Flaherty that some clarity began to appear. Suddenly the light began to peak through the storm clouds.

With John I felt for the first time ever, that there was some way out. He boiled down my life into a beautiful simplicity: "Love yourself and be committed to the natural joy that already is yours to be lived." "Don't fret over the past, or even the future." "Don't miss life. It's happening right now. Not tomorrow, not yesterday. Now." Within days of accepting this powerful realization, the weight of how I'd been trying to live my life lightened. In fact it got to the point where I forgot about my "problems" a lot of the time. I began to enjoy every moment and I still do today. Now, I would never say this is some miracle cure and my life is all sunshine and roses. My old ways still bite back, but now I have a way of processing any pitfalls, any angst. Just knowing that this new found perspective is possible to me has given me a clear way to move forward in life. Without doubt, it is the most empowering teaching I've come across in all my years of being. I not only live by its life-changing message, it makes me happy to be able to confidently share it with others."

CHAPTER FIVE

The change you seek is more than the addictions you are ready to leave behind

At the center of your being you have the answer;
you know who you are and you know what you want.

—Lao Tzu

You know very well from personal experience, how illogical your addictive behaviors are. There is no logic, no rationale or reasoning to them. They cannot, therefore, be solved by the logical reasoning mind. Einstein has reminded us that:

"Insanity is doing the same thing over and over again and expecting different results"

In the same vein he also reminds us:

"You cannot solve a problem from the same kind of awareness that created it in the first place"

Mainstream recovery program methods to *break, fight, eliminate,* or, *overcome,* addictions are all attempting to do so with the inappropriate tools of logic and analysis. Even contemporary methods still believe totally in the *problem* and give far too much attention and energy to it. Judgment is the one same ingredient at the core of all those approaches and you are living testimony that it would be mere folly to keep giving energy to things you really know just don't work.

You are also aware how equally illogical it is to expect your addictive behaviors to change unless you, the creator of them, also make change. Whether or not you have regarded your repetitious behavior as insane, as Einstein suggests, is for you to decide, but they are certainly not going to bring about the freedom your heart has always been looking for. A different *starting place* is required. Heart, not head! Your head may regularly forget to remember that, but your heart does not. The resolution for the change you desire is contained in the second of the two life-wisdoms I have selected from Einstein:

"You cannot solve a problem from the same kind of awareness that created it in the first place"

In other words, you either expand your conscious awareness to become grander than the originally perceived problem or, you simply *slip out* from the problem as you originally perceived it. Your addiction has only been created as the insurmountable problem it now seems to be, for as long as you have been approaching it from the same kind of awareness that made it so in the first place.

Everything you attract into your life is proportionate to the dominant thoughts and beliefs (judgments), that you carry.

From your new way of looking at your old ways of looking at your life, the more consciously you will observe that it is not a question of what you need to *do* to overcome them. Instead, you can transcend your addictions, you can go beyond them. No one said it better or more succinctly than Shakespeare when he reminded us, *"What's done is done."* If your thoughts are always on what has been, even if you truly detest the way things have been and the things you have done, then you will continue acting on those thoughts. What always has been can only continue to be part of your life experiences, because you are the one continuing to create them. You are the one continuing to energize them into the present. You do this of course, because you have become so attached to them, they have become part of the *story* you tell about yourself, they have become your learned behavior. Your attachment to them *is* infact your addiction. The more you look into your past and put your energy there, even if you find it reprehensible, and then continue to act on those thoughts and behaviors in exactly the same way, you produce more and more of what has always been. You are a living magnet. Everything you attract into your life is proportionate to the dominant thoughts and beliefs (judgments), that you carry. Observe, watch, see and feel which dominant thoughts are still energizing the *story* of yourself taken from your past and playing out in your present. For as long as you remain caught up in these thoughts, or refuse to give them up, you treat them as real. You keep the past, which is dead, energized as the present. So watch. Be alert. Be aware. Know in your heart that everything of the past has simply brought you to today. No judgment is required. If you don't have a story about yourself, you won't have to try living up to it. If you are not living that which is now passed, the past, it does not exist. It cannot exist.

MAKING THE UNREAL YOUR REAL AND THE REAL YOUR UNREAL. In *transcending* your addictions, that which was once made so real, now becomes unreal. That which once dominated, now disappears. That which seemed so problematic and insurmountable, now dissolves. Once you were lost and now, in the NOW, you are found. Your heart has found what your head has not been able to *do* for you. It is reminding you ... don't forget to re-member, you are infinitely greater than your thoughts would otherwise have you THINK you are!

Be aware of this discovery, for it paves the way to yet another of the great universal truths you were not taught when you first came into the world ...

You cannot NOT create

Everything you energize, past, present or future is a creation, whether it is by your thoughts, your beliefs, your words, your behavior or your actions. Be aware that you can spend your life creating chaos, or your can spend your life creating magnificence, but ... you cannot NOT create.

This is all you that you have to become aware of:

> *What is it you are creating and
> how have you been creating it?*

If there is something that feels *in tune* with your Self, save it. If it feels *out of tune* with your Self and only familiar to your learned version of yourself, delete it. That's how powerful you are!

There's a fascinating scientific experiment which nicely illustrates how you grew up to be the limited *upside-down* version of yourself. It illustrates too how you have created all you have been creating along the way ...

Researchers placed newborn kittens in experimental environments that had no vertical lines; only to find weeks later, that when the same kittens were then transferred to a normal environment, they could not see any object with a vertical dimension. For example, they could not see a chair or table with legs. As a result, the kittens kept bumping their noses into the chair or table legs until they discovered they could re-adjust their vision and expand their awareness to accommodate the new found phenomena of vertical lines. Prior to the kittens receiving their harsh awakening, anything that had not been brought into their awareness, simply did not exist. As soon as that was changed, everything changed; perception changed, limitations changed, expectations changed, freedoms changed and the frequency of sudden bumps on the nose changed. Awareness of all things once judged impossible and unknown, suddenly became very possible and newly known.

EXPANDING YOUR CONSCIOUS AWARENESS. Your life is about expanding your own awareness and my message to you is the equivalent of the bump on the nose the kitten's received in their awakening. There's so much more to you and to your life than your limited version of it has been able to demonstrate. As you expand your possibilities, everything expands. You were introduced to only a very limited version of YOU and without the awareness of a grander experience of your Self, you have continued to remain within the confines of that restrictive introduction. The change you are seeking is not simply to leave your addictive behaviors behind. Whether you knew it or not, you have been all the time seeking your Life-Source; finding your way back to your Self and inevitably becoming very confused along the way. Take heart and know that this whole unraveling process is exactly what your time on earth is all for. You have taken all the time you required to find your way home and now your heart has found what it has been looking for. The message of this book is the message you have been in search of. It's the verification of the freedom you have desired but haven't known how to grant yourself. Now your life must *be* this message and expansion, not limitation, must *be* your life.

"Addiction has been something I have encountered for as long as I can remember. I **PARDEEP'S STORY** was born into an East Indian family in Canada that consisted of my parents, sisters, grandparents, aunt, uncle and cousins. Being the first boy, there was much pressure and expectation on me from the very start.

My first experience with addiction was my father's alcoholism. I spent much of my life in fear of him. The pressures that he himself felt from his family were projected onto me and I became the target of his anger and frustration from a young age.

My own addictions began early. From a young age I found comfort in eating. This led me into a very lengthy and unhealthy relationship with food. Growing up as an overweight East Indian in a small town was not conducive to a happy and peaceful life and I spent my time in constant anxiety and fear of being bullied both at school and at home. I always knew I was different from the others around me. I preferred the company of girls; I related to them better. It was Barbies not G.I. Joes that grabbed my attention. As a child, I could not understand why I was punished for this. As the years went on, I got better at hiding signs of my sexuality, suppressing any feelings I might have, leaving me always confused, embarrassed and ashamed.

By this time, I had started to experiment with alcohol and pot: habits which quickly became an easy way to forget, not feel, be calm. This was the beginning, from which point I moved on through most substances, eventually becoming a heavy user of cocaine. Cocaine became a crutch and a distraction which I used to help me mask the emotional pain I was constantly suffering.

I came to a point where I felt defeated, I thought that this was just how I was supposed to live my life, I was in chaos; living with an eating disorder and a substance addiction. It felt insurmountable and I didn't feel things could change. I had no control over my life; I had no choice but to live in the closet. I would never be accepted for who I really was. I was totally alone.

I had tried a few times to seek assistance but nothing really got through to me. I would always end up right back in the same place of chaos. My father died and things quickly spiraled. It was at that point that I agreed with my family I would again seek help. I had had enough of the feelings of anxiety, worthlessness and guilt.

I found a place of rehabilitation in a private addiction treatment center in Canada. It was there that I felt the first sense of a shift in myself. The fear began to subside as I began to feel accepted for the first time. Things started to become clear. The people I found myself crossing paths with were amazing and they met me without judgment or expectation. I felt a sense of calm wash over me and I began to trust the process I was going through.

I was blessed to have John Flaherty as my mentor. It was then that things really started to make sense for me. The greatest awakening was when I realized my "limitations" were not real and that I could break through all of them. I knew at once that I could take back control of my life.

The message I learned from John was for me to always live my own truth. Once I understood that, the transformational change began. I awoke immediately and the way that I perceived reality became clear and simple.

I forgave things that happened in the past, "that was then ... this is now". I forgave myself and gave myself permission to be free of what I thought was my life. I let go and stepped into my true Self. I was honest about who I was; I no longer needed to live a lie.

Some of the easiest and most practical tools that have made it possible to move forward have been the use of *Ho'oponopono* to forgive myself and *Emotional Freedom Technique*, a gentle "tapping" procedure on the hands and face to bring calm and balance when I'm in overwhelm. Using these has helped to bring a sense of peace and release.

When you change the way you look at things, the things you look at change. As I began to implement changes in my perspectives, immediately my relationships and circumstances began to change too. I began to treat myself with respect, kindness, forgiveness and patience and began to see a change in the way that others treated me.

Learning to live in the now made me realize that life is designed to unfold slowly and purposefully. I didn't need to constantly be pressing the fast-forward button.

I no longer found it necessary to strive for forgiveness or acceptance from others; I discovered that this is an inside job. Meditation became a crucial tool to allow me to connect, manifest, and heal. I used to have a "lack" mentality, believing that there was not enough of whatever I wanted to go around. I now learned that there is an unlimited supply of support, happiness and joy. I learned to trust myself. I learned infinite love and gratitude.

The biggest difference in my life has been the awareness I now hold. I am aware of signs, patterns of behavior, relationships and personalities. I am careful with my thoughts and words. I hear them once they are said. John helped me to realize that my consistent thoughts become my reality. One of the biggest differences and challenges has been embracing circumstances; embrace the fall because it never lasts that long. Express gratitude for the tough times as well as the good.

My beliefs in life have changed. I love myself. I had been living absorbed in a false sense of what was important: what I had, what I did, others' opinions of me, wealth, achievement, popularity, power. Now I try not to torment myself about such things. Instead, I ask, "How can I be of service?"

My understanding of addiction has changed. I used food, exercise, alcohol and drugs as a way of coping with the chaos that was caused by those very things. It was just a pattern of behavior and once I came to the understanding that this pattern only accomplished anxiety, despair, depression and stress, I asked myself, "Why would I continue to choose this?"

John taught me that "You cannot NOT create." I now understand that my "creation" can be greatness or it can be chaos, either way it is me who is creating it. Another thing that was really helpful for me to learn was that "There is no such thing as failure, only feedback." With this realization, I no longer make judgments of myself in the way I used to. I love knowing that joy is simply a choice.

CHAPTER SIX

Slipping out from your addictions

*Learn to ... be what you are, and learn to resign
with a good grace all that you are not.*

–Henri-Frédéric Amiel

The path that life is now inviting you to take and which is coming to you through the message of this book, belongs to an entirely different level of conscious awareness to the one from which you have been functioning. Its invitation begins with a different understanding and from a different starting place. As a result, it will only be recognized and be accepted by those who are ready to receive its liberating message.

If you know in the depths of your heart, that there must be more to life, your life, than your experience of it has been so far. If you know that you can put your hand on your heart and sincerely answer *"Yes"* to the all important question: *"Have you had enough yet?"* then you will know why life is making the invitation to you that it is and why this book has come to you at the time it has. When you are ready to give your self back to your Self, when you are ready to expand the awareness of your true nature, you are ready to be free.

If you know that you can put your hand on your heart and sincerely answer "Yes" to the all important question: "Have you had enough yet?" then you will know why life is making the invitation to you that it is and why this book has come to you at the time it has.

Again, take a nice deep breath and let out a big sigh of relief. No matter how long it has taken you to unravel your Self from the egoic self, once you have found your path, you are on your way. Things learned about you can now give way to truths about you and from these truths can come new ways of looking at life, your life. From new ways of looking at your life, you no longer view life as being something you are up against. There is no necessity to *overcome* problems, you are ready instead to *transcend* them.

TRANSCENDING YOUR ADDICTIVE BEHAVIOR. Transcending your addictions is not the same as remaining in recovery from them. Transcending your addictions is to move beyond them. To *transcend* your addictions is to no longer treat your learned behaviors with the depth of fear, or, indeed with the reverence, or the attention, or even with the same resistance, sincerity, or dedication as you have been doing. For it is only your acceptance of them, that brings them into existence. This is essential to grasp. It's so essential, I will repeat it again. Your addictions exist, only because of your acceptance of them. As you really get to the core of this truth, you begin to go free ...

> **Your addictions exist, only because of your acceptance of them.**

Other than your acceptances of them, your addictions and dependencies don't exist. They can't exist. Only your acceptance of them makes them REAL.

Similarly, always trying to avoid your addictions actually gives them energy. Other than the time you spend avoiding them, they don't exist. They can't exist. It is only the time and energy that you spend avoiding them that makes them REAL.

Your fear of your addictions feeds them and ensures that they remain present. Other than your fear of them, they don't exist. They can't exist. Only your fear and dread of them makes them REAL.

Fighting or trying to beat your addictions does not lessen your cravings because *whatever you resist will persist*. Other than your attempts to beat your addictions into submission, they don't exist. They can't exist. Only your attack on them makes them REAL.

Ignoring the implications of your addictive behaviors does not make them disappear either. Other than your constant attempts at ignoring them, they don't exist. They can't exist. For your very act of ignoring them means they have to remain evident. It makes them REAL.

A life-time devoted to recovery is the surest way for addictions to hold power over you. Only your need to be in recovery from them makes them REAL. Other than the need to be in a constant state of recovery from them, they don't exist. They can't exist. That's how powerful you are, not how power-less!

Your attempts to overcome your addictions, valiant and determined though they may have been, are a process of DOING. That, of course, is no different to the way you have always gone about life. You have spent many years living from day to day, going from action to reaction. You have been ruled by your head, acting impulsively and habitually to the programmed way your mind was conditioned and set.

THE SUFFERING OF SEPARATION. When you were *addicting* you were opting for a way that became familiar and habitual to you. Addicting is the choice most regularly made by those who wish to minimize the pain of trying to make their *upside-down* version of themselves work.

Those of you who have chosen to be "in recovery" from the fallout of your addictive behaviors are also opting to minimize your pain. Your way of doing so is by learning relapse prevention measures, attending meetings, attending counseling, therapy and the like. In effect, each option is much the same as the other. Both the person "in addiction" and the person "in recovery" is making adjustments to a life-style dominated by deep pain which, when left untended, becomes immense suffering. Each option replaces old life choices with new ones, choices that feel more comfortable or less intolerable than the other.

Prior to the point in your life that you are at now, your addictive behavior was how you escaped your anxiety, your frustration, your meaninglessness. You simply sought some intoxicant, some painkiller to do the job for you. Those of you who then adopted the various processes advocated by the recovery movement, opted for another means to do a similar job. The two options on offer look like two different things, but a lifetime, your lifetime, spent "in recovery" and a lifetime, your lifetime, spent "in addiction" are each assisting you to accomplish much the same thing: essentially they assist you to adjust to your suffering. They do not free you of it.

Each embodies the fear that for you to *have* a life you need to be forever *doing* something to prove yourself worthy of it. Both options have in common the mistaken belief that you and life are separate from one another. When you are spending every day "in addiction", you are fixated on ways of closing the mind-made gap between life and your experience of living it. When you are spending every day "in recovery" you are fixated on ways of closing the mind-made gap between feeling separate from life and your desire to be in harmony with it. Either way, it depends on what you must *do* to achieve it and, as a result, it never gets done! For as long as you live in separateness, you will always feel immense pain because of its untruth. In truth of course, it is not ever possible to be separate from the Life-Source that is sourcing you. With every inhalation and exhalation you are constantly being *life-ed*, so to speak. You are life and life is you.

> **For as long as you live in separateness, you will always feel immense pain because of its untruth.**

A NEW DEFINITION OF YOUR SELF. From the moment you were born, you embarked on a lifetime of *discovery*. You have been desperately in search of YOU, searching to *discover* your Being. Without the awareness of your Being, your very Self, *who you truly are,* you have been suffering; trying to make sense of the non-sense of life, your life. The more you have been trying to make your life work, using just one or other of only two ways known to you, the more your suffering has remained in place. Your ways of trying to make life work have been so very *trying!*

The adjustments you have made to your suffering, by whichever choice you made, still continue to make room for more suffering in your life. For adjustments are never going to be sufficient. Only by being resigned to suffering, are you continuing to keep it. Resignation to it, makes your suffering REAL. Without your act of resignation, your suffering doesn't exist. It can't exist.

There is a way beyond your suffering of course, without having to make room for it ...

Everything your head could not discover for itself is everything your heart's been looking for. My heart's intention is to assist your own heart's intention to bring its search to completion. There is no need to make your experience of life so limited. There is no need to adjust to suffering. You can be free of it.

Once you discover the truth of who you are, the separation and false-hood by which you were once trying to live your life, gives way to a new definition of yourself. For as long as you were making adjustments to cope with pain and misery in your life, whether by addictive ways or by trying to prevent it in your recovery process, you have at best been "managing" your suffering but never going beyond it. Only by knowing what you don't want, can you know what you do want, and this will always be made easier, by knowing who you are NOT.

The message of this book has reminded you to become aware of *who you are* NOT, so you can at last come to know *who you truly are*. Once you know *who you truly are*, you will be living the more complete expression of yourself. At one time that possibility seemed so far out of reach, and now, in the NOW, it has become your realization. That's how powerful you are!

NICOLE'S STORY | "After the break-up of my first marriage, which had been very abusive, I met a new partner. In time, we married and life was good. My new husband was charismatic, the life of the party, always out to have a good time.

I was in love with my new partner and had hopes of a life with children, his own from his first relationship and ours together. Marriage and a healthy balanced relationship was everything I had hoped for. Unfortunately, my new life was built on a lie right from the beginning. I started to notice that the occasional glass of wine he would have with me at dinner was turning into much more. Whenever I would mention it or confront him, he denied that his drinking was out of control. I had noticed in myself, that my weight had crept up and that my blood pressure was being affected by the amount of alcohol we were having, so I thought that I would "quit" indulging nightly and see if that would lead to some change in my husband's drinking. This was more difficult than I thought for myself and for him. We agreed to limit our consumption to less than 7 drinks per week and we would write it on the calendar. I remember him saying later that this was when he knew he was out of control. The truth was, he had already begun hiding his dependency on alcohol and was lying to me about it. It was already beyond alcohol, he was using cocaine to counter the effects of alcohol so that I wouldn't notice it when I came home from work.

He had experimented with cocaine use in his previous marriage. Lying had been his way. Going out on business events, staying out at night, being unfaithful. He had twisted the story about his "crazy" ex-wife for me to believe that it was her behavior at fault and not his. His family thought that I was "the one". I had "saved their son" from himself. I know he had changed since he met me. He was more settled and he was living a healthier lifestyle, yet they were just as fooled as I was about his honesty.

It was on our honeymoon in Phoenix that I saw the real addict come to life. We were to meet my girlfriend from elementary school for some shopping, lunch and a hockey game. Boy did that go horribly wrong. He didn't eat all day, started drinking before we left at noon, and waited for us in a nearby restaurant. He drank all afternoon, while we shopped. He was so out of control by the time the hockey game started, I sent him back to the hotel in a cab. I was embarrassed and made excuses for him. All of the co-dependent thoughts that spouses of addicts go through were going through my head: was he gonna be mad at me and so on and so on. Then I started to question myself ... we were on vacation, he hadn't eaten, I should have made sure that he had. Ultimately, I'd convinced myself that somehow his behavior was all MY fault.

When I arrived at the hotel after the game, my biggest fear came true. He was nowhere to be found. He stumbled in sometime after 4 am, ranting and raving that he hated me. How could I have done this to him? He wanted a divorce and was flying home first thing in the morning. This was not how I expected our honeymoon to end after we had some glorious days in Sedona, mountain biking, hiking, doing yoga, meditation in amongst the Red Rock Canyons and mystical vortexes. What had I got myself into?

He was drinking every day. I don't know the extent of his cocaine use, but if I look back he was working from home in those days, wining and dining clients at lunch. I know now the signs of the days that he had used to sober up, before I came home. He later confessed to me that he hadn't been going to work or participating in work at all for about three months. Instead, he would get up with me in the morning, get ready for work and pretend to check emails and make calls in preparation for his work day, until I left the house. After I left he would wait for the liquor store to open and usually he would be the first client. He knew the owner by name. Sometimes, when he had his daughters with him for the weekend, it was too much stress for him to cope with. He found it hard to deal with his ex-wife and the uncertainty of whether they would come over to see him or not. He'd take his daughters for a Slurpee at the local 7-11 store and slip next door to Harvey's liquor store, to put some alcohol in his own Slurpee. He had immense guilt over the break up of his first marriage and leaving his girls. Possibly feelings back to his own childhood.

At a later time, my husband took a leave of absence from work. They put him on short term disability. I couldn't quite grasp why, but perhaps his manager and co-workers saw more than I did. It wasn't more than three weeks of him being home that we admitted him to detox. He was so deeply depressed and addicted to his obsession with alcohol that he couldn't get out of bed. He pleaded with me to stay home and take care of him. I couldn't watch what he was doing. I kept my own work routine going as well as I could and watched the man that I loved slip away and be consumed by addiction. The family counselors just told me to go to Al-Anon for support. I did attend a few times but found it depressing. It was like going to the funeral for the living dead. Those attending had all accepted that their family members were powerless against their addictions. They had also accepted that their lives would not change either. I could not do that.

His work health benefits plan assigned a counselor who suggested that my husband go into rehab, but warned that it would take some time to get him there. I went with him a few times, he was drunk by the time I got home to pick him up for the appointments. This is when I describe the time in our life when the "wheels fell off".

Anyone looking at our relationship from the outside would think we had an amazing life style together. Each of us was making in excess of $120,000 per year. We had flourishing careers, we were just married and in our mid 30's. We vacationed all over the world two or three times a year. We were active, mountain biking, skiing, running in races, camping with friends and family. We were described by friends as a "power couple". We had a beautiful home which we completely renovated ourselves. We drove nice cars. We didn't want for much. Underneath, however, our personal life was falling apart. Three times a month we were in a counselor's office getting advice on what to do about my husband's stress over the custody of his girls. I can't describe just how much that affected me and our marriage and his drinking was becoming more and more of an issue. Now he wasn't hiding his addiction anymore. He would still lie to me about it even though it was obvious. The counselor asked that I stay home and take away his access to money, cars and alcohol. She ASKED ME TO CONTROL AN

ADDICT!!! What a joke. She asked me to do the impossible and control someone else's behavior! So, the "wheels fell off!"

One morning, while I was off work for the two week period it would take to get him into rehab, he went out for a run with our dog. I still wanted to believe his honesty. After two hours of him not returning, I panicked and starting calling his friends and his ex-wife. They all immediately got in their vehicles and went to look for him. Up until this time, I had kept his addiction a secret from our families, our friends, and our neighbours. I was naive in thinking that they didn't know or suspect that he had a drink problem. They all showed up at the house after about thirty minutes and we were sitting in the living room when he showed up with our dog. He was drunk, dirty and wet from falling into the North Saskatchewan River, trying to get some water out of that stinky slough to mix with the vodka he had purchased. It was at that moment that those present with me made an impromptu intervention. Two of his friends stayed at the house with me as he began to get violent and angry, but I knew something had to be done.

The time waiting to get into rehab were the longest two weeks of my life. My mom flew out for support and we finally got him on the plane to rehab for a thirty day program. The treatment center promised all would be great. However, it wasn't quite like that.

I did see glimpses of progress being made, since I visited every week-end, but there were still more challenges to face. I was informed that my co-dependent behavior was empowering my husband's addiction. I had to do my part, so that I could help him get better right?? I felt like I was going crazy, imagining things. I was overwhelmed, frustrated, out of control. But I still convinced myself that as long as I tried hard enough and did more, the nightmare would change. Little did I know...

I later found out that on his first evening pass from rehab, he went out with other "friends" that he had met there. They all got high. What a lie and a joke this was all turning out to be. We had paid $7,000 for my husband to go to a private residential treatment center and to recover from his alcohol addiction, only to find that he was now smoking crack! I find this so hard to take as I look back on it. I had paid half of that amount, desperate to get my husband back. His employers had paid the other half, only to fire him two months later after he showed up to work drunk again.

During that time, his ex-wife had given him her prescription meds, as he "had a sore back". He crushed them and snorted them with our kitchen equipment that I had used many times to make a lovely dinner for us. Was this behavior ever going to end?

I had spent so many lunch hours driving home to take my husband to AA meetings. I met a lot of really great people at those meetings, mostly men like my husband who told stories of their own fall from "grace". They were working feverishly now to rebuild their lives and their relationships, but none of them sounded like my husband and none of them sounded like they were me or in my situation.

When my husband was finally let go by his employer, his family attempted to intervene and get him back into the rehab program he had just finished in September. He got there, and then "escaped" from it. A missing person's report was filed and I thought, finally! I was tired, emotionally exhausted. When he eventually showed up, I told him that I just couldn't do it all again.

For the next four months we rode an emotional roller-coaster of addiction. There were temporary periods of sobriety interspersed with weekend visits into hospital emergency wards. The emergency room doctors would simply tell me and him that it was his choice to live this way. They could give him medications to get off the physical addiction and stabilize his body through prescription of Valium and Vicodin, which I had to keep on myself at all times. Otherwise, he would have taken them like they were Smarties to try to get high off them. I didn't know where to turn to.

Christmas Eve is my favourite day of the year, but it was again ruined. My husband put on a facade of not drinking and then scoured my family's home for alcohol. He found a bottle of twelve year old ice wine that my parents had saved for a special occasion. He hid in the dining room, pretending to play a board game with a friend he had met in rehab. He was hiding the wine behind my mom's long drapery. It made me very sad, embarrassed and hurt. My mom yelled at him in front of his friend. She was also embarrassed, sad and hurt. I started to see that we had been exiled from our friends and family because of his behavior. He was no longer that guy that was the life of the party but the annoying drunk that nobody wanted to have over. I was married to that. And I was no longer welcome either.

In the New Year he took up a new job offer, but it lasted only a month before he quit. I still don't know what exactly happened, but I do know that his outrageous behavior on a company trip had raised the eyebrows of the company executives.

We were to leave on a "recovery trip" to Mexico for a week, when he overdosed at home in our bed the day before we were scheduled to go. A friend of ours called 911. His lips were blue and his breathing was bad. The paramedics asked what he could have possibly taken. I told them of his alcoholism and his affinity for oxycontin. I had no idea what else he had been experimenting with.

I tried to get him admitted to the psychiatric ward for the minor threats he had made to end his life, wishing it was all over. However, after two days in Emergency he was sent home to my care. We got home and I told him I wasn't willing to live like this. I couldn't. I had cancelled the trip to Mexico and I knew I needed to get away and spend some time with my family. I left that evening and he was happy to get rid of me so that he could indulge his drinking habits again.

I never saw full bottles of vodka or white wine in our home, only the empties. It was like finding a mistress's clothes hidden around your home. I became obsessed with uncovering all of his hiding spots. There were bottles in the closet, in the office, above the cupboards in the kitchen, in the bathroom drawers. They were everywhere.

After I had enjoyed a good night's sleep at my parents, he called me sobbing, telling me he was sorry. He was admitting himself into a private rehabilitation treatment center. I was thrilled, this was it. They would help him get better, get my husband back to good. But it was at this point that I realized, even if he was sober again, things would never be the same. I paid the deposit on two of my credit cards over the phone and, within a few days, he was admitted. The center offered a thirty, sixty or ninety day program costing between $8,000 to $20,000.

Once he got sober after the first week of being there, he asked me and his mom and his sisters to all come and participate in the family program. We all agreed. However, eighteen days later, he was discharged for drinking with one of the other clients. He disappeared for about three days before calling me sobbing, asking me to book him a ticket home. He landed drunk, sad and defeated.

The next six weeks his behavior became abusive and much worse. He was openly manic and feeding his addiction. He came home from one of his "secret" trips to the liquor store with a 4ft tall stuffed giraffe and another time with a $120 pair of neon yellow running shoes for me that I would never have dreamt of wearing. I can laugh about that now!

His abusive nature caused me to store some of my precious items at my friend's house and pack an overnight bag, just in case he changed the locks as he kept threatening to. He'd become abusive to the cat and I began to sleep in our guest room downstairs as he would wake up in the night raging at me and yelling nonsense. His unpredictable behavior frightened me and reminded me of my previous husband who was very abusive and intimidating towards me.

It was my dad's 60th birthday and I was flying to Vancouver for the weekend. Hard as it was to leave my husband behind in the state that he was in, I felt I had to make this decision. I remember kissing him as I left him in bed as I set off for work with my weekend luggage. Little did I know that would be the last time. I had booked an appointment that same weekend to see John Flaherty for the first time. I needed some answers. I didn't know what to do. Where to turn.

The other two counselors I had seen over the past few years, plus the countless hours of research and numerous admittance clerks I had spoken to at detox units, emergency wards, rehab centers did not have the answer to how I could get my husband sober and have him stay that way. Little did I know that this long weekend in 2010 would pivotally change not my husband's way of life, but my own! My quest had already begun with some of the books that I had been reading in the past few months with the teachings of Eckhart Tolle and Melody Beattie. However, nothing prepared me for the work that was about to begin with John.

I had an amazing birthday celebration with my dad, I realized that I had given up being close to my family and I was struggling to hold onto a second failed marriage. How could this be, when I was so successful in every other part of my life? I had been an honor roll student, beauty pageant princess in my small hometown, I was vice president of the student body. A born leader in everything I did. University graduate, top of my sales team at work. I come across as confident, smart, passionate, outgoing, driven and together. How was I facing this crisis? My husband was out of control, I didn't know what to do to fix it. My life had become crazy.

John listened to my "story". I described the crazy life that I had been living for the past year and half or so and how much things had escalated. So the big question for me from John, was "Have you had enough yet, Nicole? Have you had enough?" I thought about it for about two seconds. I whispered, "Yes. I don't want to live this way. That's why I am here."

John explained that by admitting that fact, I had already discovered the answer. I had exhausted myself over the past two years, trying to find an alternative answer, a compromise. There wasn't one. "If you don't want to be just dying to live," John said, "then the answer is ... don't!"

I had made it my life's work to research addiction, rehab and how to be a loving and supportive wife. I came to realize that my husband's addiction could only be cured by one thing ... HE HAD TO MAKE HIS CHOICE ABOUT HIS LIFE. That was it. Nothing I did, or wished, or tried to control, or influence could change another person. Becoming a better wife, a nicer person or going to church (which I also tried) would change things in my husband's life. I had tried everything I could, even high dose vitamins while his mother tried holy water!

The switch flipped during my first three hour mentoring session with John. I had an "ah-ha!" moment. I knew that I had "had enough" and that I was not prepared to continue participating in living a life "dying" alongside an addict, even if he was my husband.

I spent the rest of the weekend at my sister and brother in law's house. I exchanged some irrational text messages with my husband and when I called home, he refused to answer. I knew what I needed to do. I called my friend and she agreed to meet me at the house. Her husband would meet me with a pick-up truck and help me move my things out. I did not know where I was going to, but I tried to remain brave. It was the only decision I had control of. How did "I" want to live my life? LIVING ... this was my first step.

I spent the day living with the most important things to me in my vehicle, my cat, my dog and a few memorable things from my grandparents, and such. It is truly humbling to realize that all you need is a very small amount when it really comes down to it. I knew of a friend who was looking for a roommate. I called her and asked if I could move in with her. She agreed.

In the meantime, my husband had once again checked himself into rehab. He would be gone for ninety days this time and so I moved back into the house. This time, I refused to pay for any of his treatment. He needed to pay it out of his RSPs or his severance. Again, I found out that he had spent that money already, including the RSPs. After moving back into the house I started cleaning up the disgusting mess of vomit, empty wine and vodka bottles, shrimp tails, and watermelon. It was like junkies had been squatting in my living room for the past week. It felt good to be home though, even under the circumstances and on my terms.

I stood my ground in the coming weeks, telling my husband when he called that I wanted a separation. I wanted to sell the house and part ways. He agreed begrudgingly. He thought he would get sober and we could reconcile. I was not willing to return to life under those conditions.

The financial disaster that our household affairs were in soon became apparent. My husband had not paid any of our utility bills for months ($1000), nor had he paid our house taxes for the past two years ($5,000) and luckily I found the notice from the City. They were about to sell our home at auction for the taxes. I found that he had spent all of the $20,000 in severance, his $100,000 in RSPs that he had when we first moved in together. I had paid for half of his first rehab $3,300 and the $8,000 for the failed second attempt. His parents loaned him another $18,000 for the ninety day program. I had no choice but to cash in my own investments to pay off these debts.

He left treatment after sixty days or so. He never went back to finish his ninety day stay and soon his life began to spiral out of control. I heard sporadic stories of women, car wrecks, his driver's license revoked, spending the insurance money on a month in Puerto Vallarta, in and out of the hospital, a stroke ... on and on and on ...

I still received random phone calls and text messages. It wasn't until I served him with divorce papers and he signed them that the crazy communication finally stopped. All those midnight phone calls, pleading with me and stirring up guilty feelings came to an end.

I struggled with so much guilt after making the choice to live my life LIVING instead of making the choice to live my life DYING. I had made a vow through sickness and in health to stand by my husband. He forced me to make the decision of either him or me. I chose ME and Life. He was not going to take that from me.

Over the next two years I continued to attend mentoring sessions with John. He helped me work through and understand why I was continuing to enter into intimate relationships which always contained so much drama, addiction and with men whom I could not depend upon. I also discovered where there had been unresolved issues with my dad. I started to understand the various forms of addiction and began weeding out the root cause of my repetitive cycle. I was able to draw healthy boundaries between myself and my family. I began letting go of friends who drained me and I learned to let go of the need to control, which is the most freeing thing of all! Now I know how to feel "deserving".

I was 39, single and on my own. Hardly how I had imagined my life. I thought I would have started a family by now and my time was ticking away. I started casually dating again and began to rebuild my life on my own. LIVING. I used this time to figure out what I wanted and what I did not want in a partner. It was amazing to me how the things I didn't think were such a big deal, really were! This was the first time in my adult life that I had lived on my own. I had nobody to answer to. I took a month long trip to Thailand with a girlfriend to re-charge and to gain new perspective. It was so cathartic.

With the proceeds of the divorce, I purchased my own home and made it my own. I continued to evolve and tried to become loving and not bitter because of my experience. I worked very hard to feel empathy and love towards my ex-husband and grateful for the experience that I had had with him. Eventually my anger and sadness did turn to peace, empathy and gratitude. I did not want to become bitter, jaded and angry at the world for what I had experienced. It was a lot of hard work, but I feel that I have succeeded.

Finally, just when I had stopped searching for a new companion, I met an amazing man. Everything I could have wished for (and a little bit more!) We have open communication inside of a loving, respectful relationship. We travel and enjoy an active life together.

My life has turned 180 degrees. Every single day for the past three years, I have made deliberate choices to change my life. Finally, my personal relationship matches the other "together" aspects of my life."

CHAPTER SEVEN

You are Energy

Your burden is of false self-identifications—abandon them all.

–Nisargadatta Maharaj

Everything is energy. The physical world is nothing but a slower vibration of energy. The non-physical is present, but not visible to the physical plain, for its movement is at a much quicker vibration. Energy is the prime mover of all we see and know. Everything that we encounter has a vibrational frequency and a movement to it. If you look at the page of this book through a very powerful microscope you would see molecules, atoms, electrons sub and sub-atomic particles moving about in ceaseless energy patterns. The book appears solid to your eyes only because your senses, which also vibrate, perceive solidity at this frequency.

In the same way, everything is in a state of motion. Even though, to the slowed down frequency of your physical form, it may seem that you are sitting very still in this moment, the planet is spinning once every twenty four hours, orbiting the sun once every 365 days and moving through space at fantastic speeds. Everything has an energy field and, depending on the frequency and vibration of its movement, it will impact you and the rest of the physical plain you inhabit accordingly.

When you are in a negative emotion of fear, depression, anxiety, helplessness or aloneness you are vibrating a slower speed than when you are in your heightened state of natural joy.

Illness, disease and disharmony all vibrate at the slowest frequency, as do your fears, your anxieties, depression and of course your addictions. It will feel this way to your body too, as you will have experienced when you have been burdened and in overwhelm. In the faster, but still slow vibration, ordinary human awareness resides. Then there is the much quicker vibrations that make up the high energy of conscious awareness. Your *e-motions* are literally your energies—in—motion. When you are in a negative emotion of fear, depression, anxiety, helplessness or aloneness you are vibrating at a slower speed than when you are in your heightened state of natural joy. When you are in a high level of natural joy, your body feels *in tune* with the rest of life. When you are in a negative state, your moods drop and your body feels the same drop in synchronicity with it. It feels *out of tune*. All positive change is made when you are functioning at the faster energy frequency and movement of conscious awareness.

As you become the "observer", rather than the "do-er", you shift your energy field from the lower to the higher vibrational frequencies. You enter the non-physical state and affect change at the physical level. Meditation is the same practice. It is the way of creating an energy field of receptivity, so that solutions to challenges your head could not find for you can be picked up by your heart from the non-physical plain. Answers to your perceived problems always exist but often remain invisible from you, depending on the frequency of the energy vibration at which you are functioning.

WHEN YOU ARE UP AGAINST LIFE. While you have been functioning at the lower state frequency of addiction, you were resonating with the inner view that you were separate from everything and everyone else. It then feels like you are up against life. At the higher frequency you feel your connectivity with all of life, there is no sense of separation from it. Your body also feels in alignment with the choices you make, the thoughts you think, the emotions you feel and the words you choose to define your presence.

The learned version of you, the ego-self, will have been vibrating from the lower energized frequency. The environment you were born into, the early influences, attitudes, pervading thoughts, beliefs and behaviors you experienced, set the level of expectation you began to believe was the only available way for you to function. No matter how loving your parents may have been, no matter how often they said, *"You know we only want what's best for you."* Their best, is still going to play second fiddle to the truth of all you are. I believed, like many others, that I had the best parents in the world, albeit with the limited resources they had at their disposal. In other words, the best our parents give to us is precisely that, *their best.* It is not the Source of life sourcing you. Rather, it's more true to say that the impact and influence of parents, the environment you were born into and the expectations that formed your early childhood development, became

> ... the impact and influence of parents, the environment you were born into and the expectations that formed your early childhood development, became the emerging personality you began to THINK was you.

the emerging personality you began to THINK was you. This is the ego and it vibrates at the same energy level and frequency as the environment and the expectations you continue to identify yourself with.

The ego is the mis-identification of your true Self. It is the accumulation of beliefs and limitations you have collected about yourself as you have gone through life and it is also the energy level from which that belief has been functioning. When people use the term ego, they most readily think of it as meaning an inflated self importance. The ego, however, can actually keep a person very small in life, insignificant, almost invisible. This is most often the case when the belief collected about a person's self-worth has been diminished by others. Again, the energy level that the ego functions from, when such a low vibrational belief is held, is proportionate to the belief itself. The physical form of the person holding such low self-worth literally does go unseen, it is insignificant to others, it remains invisible to more dominant ego personalities. You will know exactly what I mean, if you have been existing almost as an apology for life, rather than the unique and powerful presence you *truly are.*

THE IMPRINT YEARS. Everyone has an ego. Your persona that was shaped and formed about yourself, particularly before the age of 7 years, by the people, places and things you encountered and then interpreted as yourself,

> **The ego is not who you are, it is who you have learned to become—who you THINK you are and who you THINK other people THINK you are.**

is the ego. The ego is not who you are, it is who you have learned to become—who you THINK you are and who you THINK other people THINK you are. That is why those first 7 years are known as the imprint years. It is the period in which you began to forget to re-member your true essence, replacing it instead with the made-up "self" you learned to create *about* YOU. As you were being shown how to *do* life you forgot to remember how to *be* it and you have been living this *upside-down* version of life ever since.

Before the age of 7, you spent much of your time in play, where the imaginary and the real world were mixed and became one and the same, without separation. Throughout your imprint years, you had not developed the capacity to rationalize or reason. As a result, your perceptions of the world were directly down-loaded into your unconscious mind, without question. Only later, did you begin to develop your analytical conscious mind to filter and discriminate that which your unconscious mind was efficiently storing in its memory-bank *about* you and *about* life. The implications of this process are vital for you to grasp, for it is in those seven years that you were *programmed* and *conditioned*. It was in this time-frame that you learned to behave and react to external events and to internal thoughts and emotions, in the way you are still conditioned to do today. It was in this stage of your development that you started to function from a particular energy level; one that was either a faster moving and a more consciously aware understanding of your unique presence and worth, or one that functioned from a low energy vibrancy of inadequacy or low self-worth.

The identity you formed about your Self was a whole mixed bag of impacts and influences that went unquestioned by you and which formed the ego-self. It is no surprise that the Jesuits, aware of the programmable imprint years, were to make their bold claim:

"Give us a child until it is six or seven years old and it will belong to the Church for the rest of its life."

They knew that once a child's programming was imprinted with its dogmas and its teachings, it would remain unconsciously imprinted and continue into adulthood to be expressed as a behavior for the rest of life.

The perceptions and beliefs about your life that you formed in your imprint years have become your unequivocal truths. They have also formed the "story" you have created; who you have come to THINK you *are* and who you THINK other people THINK you *are*. Although you have continued to develop your more critical thinking conscious mind since the age of seven, your unconscious memory-bank of stored data is still feeding you with its imprinted mixed bag of downloaded perceptions. Your learned egoic self is still habitually operating from your store of memory and will continue to do so, unless you make the active effort to reprogram your unconscious thought pattern.

When life for you is just not working, when it seems you are taking one step forward and always at least two back, it's vital to *discover* the predominant unconscious belief that is still running the show. Only by elevating your conscious awareness, will you return yourself to your Self, speeding up your slower energy vibration.

As you have downloaded any limiting or fearful sabotaging beliefs about yourself, your programming has simply continued to replay them. Who you learned to become and how you *pieced your life together* will either be working well for you today or, it will not. In either case, it is but a pale reflection of who you truly *are*. The downloaded imprints, stored unconsciously, have become interpreted by you as your truths. They have been invisibly generating your behaviors, both the wanted and the unwanted ones.

Let me give you an example ...

There are only two experiences of fear that a human being instinctively possesses: the fear of falling and the fear of loud noises, all other fears are learned, they are acquired. So, as you emerged from your mother's birth canal, you instinctively knew how to move through it, how to swim. Yet, when you first encountered swimming as an infant you automatically pick up on the adult fears. Their fear for your safety immediately registers in your unconscious memory bank and is translated by you that water is something to be feared. At once the trauma of the water being life threatening completely overrides the formerly instinctual ability you had to swim. Suddenly the experience now becomes, not how well you can swim, but, how best to survive the threat of drowning.

In this same way, the whole of your identity is formed. Through your developmental experiences you increasingly acquire a fear of life itself and create the perception that you are a weak, frail, vulnerable being, always under threat, always in separation from life itself. Not surprisingly, the threat of addiction has falsely been treated with the same degree of fear.

Traditional and even conventional addiction recovery programs, while encouraging many people to make adjustments to their dependencies, still remain bound by limiting beliefs. As a result, the discipline and conditions required of those who wish to remain free of addictions, never fully calls forth that which the addicted person most yearns to experience again; the freedom to experience themselves as they truly are.

LIKE ATTRACTS LIKE. The more you hold a belief about your eternal need to be "in recovery", the more dependent on your dependency you remain. The more dependent you remain, the more your judgment of yourself continues to function at a low energy vibration. The lower the energy vibration, the more people, places and things of a similar vibration you attract into your life. The more you attract of the same, the more difficult it is for you to perceive the possibility of any other way of living.

For the last 25 years, I have had the privilege of assisting many people to move through their addictions to a life fully lived and fully expressed as their own truth. I have traveled the globe spending time in North America, Europe, India and Africa and in that time I have met countless people who have told me that they were now "in recovery". On every occasion, I have asked the same three questions:

"What are you in recovery from?"
"How long will it take to recover?"
"How will you know when you've ever recovered?"

Amazingly enough, my questions draw nothing more than a mystified look and a totally silent response. People have become so accustomed to identifying themselves as their perceived need, that they have lost sight of their true nature. Identification with addictive behavior, dependency, separateness and the fear of not being accepted unless they maintain attachment to their identification, is actually *who* they have come to THINK they *are*. The possibility of living without this life-time imposed sentence has not even been fully considered. As a result, it remains as an impossibility to them.

People have become so accustomed to identifying themselves as their perceived need, that they have lost sight of their true nature.

DETACHMENT. The mainstream ways of recovery from addiction belong to the same erroneous mentality as the made-up identity you originally created and accepted about yourself. Namely, that your addiction is real, rendering you powerless, and that any expectations you may have beyond that are unreal. For as long as you decide to remain attached to such a limited way of experiencing your world, you become pitted against your addictions. Once you believe yourself to be up against your addictions, you energize them and they become REAL. The more you remain the victim of your beliefs, the more you continue to function from your slower energy vibration. A lifetime spent overcoming addictions is a lifetime being attached to them. Other than the attention you give to them, they cannot exist.

A lifetime spent overcoming addictions, is a lifetime being attached to them. Other than the attention you give to them, they cannot exist.

Only by detaching yourself from the ego-identification you had formed about yourself, whether it be to your addictive behaviors or, indeed to your recovery process, can you raise your vibrational frequency and return yourself to your Self. Only by detaching from all you have made-up about yourself and about your life, can you be free.

For those of you who have settled for making adjustments to your suffering, not knowing it was possible to transcend it, contemplate this wise story below. When you have read the story, see what in your life you have been hanging onto so preciously. Making recovery from your addictions may be valued by you, but be crystal clear about what it is that you are more truly recovering from. Be aware how much of yourself is still feeling the need to be identified with your past. Your discovery is your freedom and your freedom is in making the return to your Self that you have so much been desiring. Here is the ultimate way to go free of your own made up *story* that you have become so attached to:

A Spiritual Master once spoke to his disciple:

"A miser decided to hide his gold in a hole at the foot of a tree in his garden. Everyday, when nobody was looking, he would pull out the gold and gaze at it. A thief saw him, went at night and robbed the gold. The following day, the miser discovered that the hole was empty and the gold gone. He got a terrible shock, but the very shock brought him to his senses and freed him from his fever for gold. He thought to himself, "Seeing this empty hole each day, has the same effect on me as seeing the gold. At last, I am a free man." So, from that day on, he would go every day to visit the empty hole at the foot of the tree and to celebrate his own liberation. With that, he became just as obsessed with visiting the empty hole every day as he had been previously obsessed with the gold. Except that, now, there was no robber to liberate him from this new and more subtle fever."

The disciple replied, *"But Master, I have already detached myself from everything!"*

"Now," replied the Master, *"detach yourself from your detachment!"*

CHAPTER EIGHT

Allowing your preference to become your reality

The alcoholic is the fellow who is trying to get his religion out of a bottle, when what he really wants is unity within himself ...

—Bill W.

Transcending addictions is the process of discovery, it is nothing to do with learning how to rid yourself of unwanted behaviors, in the ways you have been trying to do so. It is nothing to do with absorbing information or learning how to *do* anything differently in order to gain and maintain your sobriety. It is nothing to do with committing yourself to a lifetime spent in *recovery* mode.

If you were to spend another moment trying to make work that which clearly does not work, and going about it in the same way you have always tried to make it work, it won't work!

Yet, mainstream approaches to addiction recovery have still not become aware of their inadequate approach.

Let me explain ...

Trying to solve the problem of your addiction requires you to believe that such a thing as a *problem* even exists. What do you mean by the word *problem?* If you mean, something which seems insurmountable, what makes it so? If you mean something which brings pain, what keeps it so? Only a belief has that power. It's not the *problem* that holds power, it is the belief you have attributed to it. When a *problem* brings pain, your belief requires the resulting pain to be greater than you can bear. Otherwise you would not recognize it as a problem. It also requires your belief to believe that once there is pain, it will always remain. Otherwise it would not seem so insurmountable. When pain remains insurmountable, you then experience suffering: never-ending pain that you cannot bare.

Your belief then tells you that when such a never-ending condition exists, you are rendered helpless against it. That is not a fact of course, it is a belief and has become the *story* of judgment you tell about it. Your addictive behavior and your recovery is the story *about* your verifiable belief about life, your life.

The more you imagine, visualize and verbalize your belief, your story becomes the never-ending story. The more you tend to it, explain it, share it, complain about it, voice it; the more you attract evidence for it. Why? Because like attracts like, it is one of the laws of the universe and the laws of the universe are just how life works. You cannot argue with that. Like the law of gravity, it just *is*. Now the *is*, that just *is*, is that you have unwittingly become the *story* of your perceived problem. Those you meet, ask about your problem and you speak of your life *as* your problem. Your *belief* has made you and your problem one and the same thing.

In other words, that which you have selected and have become so identified with, will always remain until you no longer identify yourself *as* the problem. There cannot be a problem in your life, without you identifying it as such. No identification, no judgment. No judgment, no belief. No belief, no problem.

Einstein leaves us to deduce the obvious ... for the problem to disappear, it requires a different starting place to the one which created it.

"You cannot solve a problem from the same kind of awareness that created it in the first place"

Stop identifying yourself as your addiction!

You have been mistakenly thinking you were just a body. You had forgotten to re-member the pure potential you truly *are* and momentarily believed yourself to be all the things your unconscious mind had stored in its memory bank *about* you ...

Slip out from your mistaken identity, release judgment and go free.

The more you accept who you truly *are*, the less you need to defend beliefs about your *mistaken identity*. The moment you make that choice, you are no longer in resistance to all that just is. The moment you let go of resistance, you feel less stress. The moment you are relieved of stress, you are relieved of the pain of it. Without pain, see if you still have that which you called "problem", or ... has it disappeared?

A belief is only a thought you continue to think, much as suffering is only a pain you continue to hold. When your beliefs cease to match all that you perceive and instead begin to match all that you would prefer, then your preference must become your reality. It is law. You know that to be true, for your ready-made evidence of it is in that which you once believed to be a problem. That too became your reality. Your deep-seated belief attracted it to you over and over and over again. That which you resist persists and that which you think and believe, you attract as your reality. Just as the law of gravity says, *"that which goes up must come down,"* the law of attraction says, *"where attention goes, energy flows."* Equipped with this new discovery, let your new verifiable law of life from this day forward be:

The energy and attention I once gave to a problem, I now give to that which I declare to be the truer expression of my grander Self. I now allow my preference to become my reality and attract only to me, that which is more fully reflective of *who I truly am.*

You have been living in a small corner of your being, the tiny conscious mind and from the ego-self that intellectually rationalizes and reasons everything that is made known to it. It is as if you have been living in the porch of a mansion thinking it is all there is, forgetting that you have a whole expanse to make as your home. My intention is to make you more aware of your pure potential.

Watch *everything* you do. Whenever you forget to remember to be watching, just watch again. No need to be hard on yourself for forgetting. To forget is natural because watching is new. Then watching becomes natural and forgetting will be new. There is no time to be spent being regretful about forgetting to re-member. That is judgment and, for the one who is consciously aware, it is not necessary to spend time and energy being repentant.

AWAKENING. Discovery comes by becoming more consciously aware, by regaining clarity—not of anything you have done wrong, but, on all that had never been right— of the *who* you learned to be. Once you have that degree of clarity, the rest of your life becomes a constant discovery; a moment by moment revelation and the *only* way of looking at your life.

This discovery is the process of awakening and you cannot be half hearted about life's invitation to be awake. You can't afford to spend a lifetime in recovery mode. That's to be just so-so about your Being. You cannot spend a moment longer on your addictions or on your recovery from them.

Transcending your addictions, becoming more consciously aware, happens only when you put your total energy into it. It is to be in your conscious and in your unconscious, your waking and your sleeping, until you only see yourself elevating your presence and expanding your awareness.

"My first encounter with addictions | **MATTY'S STORY**
began when I was a child. I recall being what
I would call, "addicted" to my emotions at an early age, perhaps 7 or 8.
When I think back now, I remember being very sensitive to the extreme
highs and lows of life as a child. I was not consciously aware of it then but
I sure knew what felt good and what did not.

I would listen to a song twenty, maybe thirty or even more times,
until I couldn't stand it any more. I would drink as much cola as I could get
my hands on to feel the sugary high. It was not until much later and after
addictions to cocaine, alcohol, marijuana, OxyContin, Percocet, Ketamine,
mushrooms and other substances that I realized my addictions were not
limited to a specific area. I was not just a drug addict but a food addict and,
in general, a fully blown, out of control, all-encompassing energy vampire!
Nothing was ever enough. I needed to feel high all the time, by whatever
means necessary.

Once I started drinking at age 13, I was hooked immediately. I rarely
drank socially, my goal always being to get as drunk as possible. I started
using marijuana at about seventeen and enjoyed that to an extreme until
about the age of 21. Cocaine came in a year or so later and never left my
side. It became a best friend. I was almost 32 when I began to feel like my
"friend" was betraying me.

I depended on cocaine to get me through the lows of life. It offered
an escape; it offered a reset button. After the hangover, I felt better; it
relieved me of stress.

My addictive behaviors were borne out of an unhappy family life. I
guess I know my mother cared for me but I never got from her the valida-
tion or the reassurance I needed. I never felt good enough for her. I never
felt accepted for who I was. There was always pressure to be something
or someone other than I was.

At one point during the years of substance abuse, my brother kicked me out of my own home, after I had mismanaged the finances resulting in serious monetary problems.

Over the years, I have left a trail of destruction in my path. Women and friends, some of whom I considered best friends, have been lost. My business, too, had to be let go of.

I was in two rehabilitation programs within two years both of which led me back to where I started. I was not committed at that time and without the commitment, I was never going to make it work. It didn't feel good to believe that nothing was going to "cure" me. It felt terrible to be in this state. I wanted to change. The late nights, the drink-driving near misses, the wrecked cars and wrecked relationships were not worth the hangovers. I believed I could leave it behind but as soon as I got back home from rehab and family tensions began again, I was straight back into my regular routine. At this point, that meant a drug and alcohol binge every two days; back and forth on alcohol and cocaine, one to counter the effects of the other. Most days I would work a full day after the binge, having had no sleep.

At this point, I began to feel a change happening within me. I could not live like this anymore. I had sought counseling assistance in the past but was never fully honest with anyone. I realized I had to do something and tried again to do so at a new rehabilitation center.

I had a wonderful girlfriend at the time who supported me and stayed with me through everything. I asked her to be there for me. I had no one else, at least that's how I felt. That is how I had felt all my life. I turned to my brother for the money for the rehabilitation center; it was very expensive and I am so grateful for his contribution to my journey.

Once in rehab I met some great people. There was a specific pair of souls I found to be the two most attractive people I have ever met. They listened to me without judgment and with complete understanding. Their names were John and Anne Louise Flaherty.

John and Anne Louise helped me to allow positive change in my life. I am so grateful that I was able to open up to their messages, owing to the great clarity with which they speak.

John challenged me everyday. He taught me to "watch" my words and to "expand" my mind. I remember the day he told me to imagine I was sitting beneath a tree: a massive and beautiful tree with sixty-five thousand leaves on it, a leaf for every thought I would have in the course of a day. All day long these leaves would fall off the tree and I had the choice of which ones I would like to catch hold of and which ones I'd like to let go of. The message from this story is that I have the power to choose. I practice this visualization almost every day of my life.

The truth that began to resonate with me was that I was in need of a complete spiritual overhaul and I was ready. I soaked up every word and every meditation session. Honestly, I learned so much about myself and experienced some almost out of body experiences that I find very hard to put into words. I'll try and tell you about my first meditation; one I will never forget. It was with Anne Louise. She put on the sounds of *Tibetan Singing Bowls*. After being shown how to relax and breathe properly, I was able to control my thoughts with pictures in my mind. I slipped into a state where I was in full control of the movie that was now playing in my mind. I felt like I was free as a bird. I was able to fly and control where I went. It was amazing! It seemed as if I was out for maybe five minutes but forty minutes had elapsed. This experience will always be valued. I will never forget it.

Now I know how to find the inner peace and acceptance that I'd spent my whole life looking for."

CHAPTER NINE

As conscious awareness expands, addictions dissolve: your heart will show you the way

Your vision will become clear only when you look into your heart.
Who looks outside, dreams.
Who looks inside, awakens.

–Carl Jung

As you become more consciously aware, your head will be governed by your consciousness and supplied by your awareness. Only then will you discover the remedy you have been looking for and redress the imbalance there has been in your life. In making your new discovery, your head has to fall into alignment with your heart and until it does, confusion will arise. Your head will not be able to work out how to continue governing you when it has only ever learned how to *do* life by living someone else's version of it. That is a little play that will go on in your head for a while. Gradually, it will get used to not ruling the roost, however, not without making every effort to cunningly edge its way back into the driving seat. Be on alert. Be aware. Be the observer.

Your body and your mind have been working in separation from your heart and as the years have gone by, they have got used to the old programming being there. For a time, the pulls of negative self-talk will arise and persist in taking you back to your old programming to support its case. Remain steadfast to your new discovery. Be the observer. Your head is like a person who has been given a new job description after a lot of years doing the original routine. It will not readily adapt to its newly defined role without creating a fuss. Your freedom and your happiness are discovered as you re-instate your Self. It is the ultimate high, once you remember who you *truly are*. As you *remember*, you will soon *realize* (see with real-eyes) ... that you have always known all there is to know about your true Self. You had just forgotten to *re-member* it.

THE PATHWAY TO YOUR BEING. From now on, your head is to receive directions from YOU, the observer Self of you, not the other way around. Your heart already knows how to serve you in this way, but until now, you have not thought it was significant. It has largely been ignored. Trust it, its time has come!

> Your freedom and your happiness is a process of *re-membering* ...
> remembering the Source of life from which you came.

There is not another thing you need to LEARN about addiction, in order to be free of it. If you never learned another thing, you would be fine because learning belongs to the head and your head can only give back to you what it has already been given. What your head is given, can only register if it is logic and ... your addictive behavior is illogical. Your addictions always have an emotional root cause to them and if you are going to address your emotions, you need to look to how you FEEL about them. That is not the function of the head, it is the domain of the heart. Hand over the way now to your heart. I assure you, your heart will instantly recognize its own way thereafter. How? Because your heart, rather than your head, is the pathway to your own Being.

New scientific discoveries being made about the heart will drastically change science, medicine and spirituality forever. Research in the new field of neuro-cardiology has now found that the central role of the heart is much more than metaphor. Your heart is constantly pumping energy and information to, from, and within, every cell of your body. Your heart has its own form of wisdom, different from that of the rational brain but every bit as important to your living, loving, working and healing.

Although most people have come to think of the brain as the level of awareness required for all things, it is a low level when compared to the heart. 5,000 times more powerful than the electro-magnetic field of the brain, your heart has the strongest electro-magnetic field of any organ in your body. It extends about 15 feet outwards and is shaped like a torus. Other people within range of it are affected by its field, the way that iron filings are affected between two magnets. It is a treasure chest of intelligence just waiting to be opened by you. There are more nerves going out from the heart to the brain than there are coming from the brain to the heart. It is also now known that when the heart, brain and body are in electro-magnetic coherence (harmony with each other), you are transported into a much, much higher level of conscious awareness. Depending on the stimuli supplied, your heart opens up to the greater spiritual ocean, to conscious awareness. The more you use your heart's intelligence, the more expanded your possibilities become. If you don't keep your heart regulated in this way, it shuts down your connectivity to the greater ocean.

KNOWING NOT THINKING. It is your heart which connects you beyond the world you have got used to living out repetitively and so unquestioningly. Your heart connects you to the greater ocean of awareness and into intuition. Of course, you will already be aware of this, for unconsciously you have quite naturally been making connectivity all of the time. Whenever you say "I just feel", your body language literally expresses your feeling simultaneously as your hand moves to hold your heart. Your body language is literally indicating from where this intelligence is coming. This is an innate intelligence. It has nothing to do with what you *learned* educationally from your parents, your school, your university or from anywhere else. That is not intelligence, that is memory, stored unconsciously. The heart is true innate intelligence, "knowing," not "thinking".

When you are drawing from your heart's intelligence, through intuition, and more intentionally through meditation, your head and heart maintain a coherence of love, appreciation, empathy, compassion, forgive-

> **Your Being is a river of intelligence, not separate from your Life-Source. It is connected to your environment, a source to be respected, co-operated and communicated with.**

ness and inner peace. If that coherence is broken with a incoherence resonance, you come out of that high state of consciousness into a lower state. In the absence of your higher state of well-being, you more readily give in to frustrations and to the emotions of fear, anger and resentment. You will know from your own experience, how it feels to be in those lower states and when and what their connection is to your addictive behavior. Your longing to seek ways of returning to the higher states is your innate desire to re-align the learned version of yourself to the coherence of who you truly *are*.

The current methodology of addiction treatment remains a very mechanical process, much in the same way as your car is taken to be repaired or serviced. Human Beings are not mechanical machinery. Your Being is a river of intelligence, not separate from your Life-Source. It is connected to your environment, a source to be respected, co-operated and communicated with.

Cardio-energetics shows that your heart, because it is a knowing, feeling, endocrine organ, acts in conjunction with your immune system and serves as its surveillance system. It senses and reacts to everything that is going on outside of you and then feeds back its findings to you. When things feel good, it lets you know and when things are not good for you, it lets you know that. The fact that cells can sense and learn has been known for much of this last century and cardio-energetics actually refers to the body having "sense-able" cells. They are constantly eavesdropping, so to speak, on your mental self-talk. Nothing that your head-chatter has been saying to itself, escapes the attention of your immune cells. Equipped with this "knowing", it is essential for you to *watch* the internal messages you are giving to your heart and to your cells. This discovery brings a radical difference to the ways you can affect change in every dimension of your being; physically, mentally, emotionally and spiritually. This discovery also brings a radical difference to the ways you must adopt, to move you beyond your addictions.

Let me explain ...

The message I am sharing with you, through the pages you have in your hands, takes you far beyond Newtonian physics, which views our existence as if it is being lived in a mechanical universe. According to the old paradigm of Newtonian physics, your body is seen as a biological machine. By tending to the parts of the "body machine" it was thought that this mechanical process would be sufficient to modify your health and behavior.

However, with the advent of quantum physics, scientists have realized the flaws in Newtonian physics. Quantum physics shows us that the invisible, immaterial realm is actually far more important than the material realm. In fact, quantum physicists have revealed that it is your thoughts that are primarily shaping the health of your physical body and indeed how you experience your reality. Therefore, seeing the body as a biological machine, in need of mechanical servicing and repair, will at best address symptoms, but is unlikely to bring about the life changes you desire.

WHERE ATTENTION GOES ENERGY FLOWS. Newtonian and mechanical in its ideology, mainstream addiction recovery regimes also mistakenly treat addictive behaviors as biological machinery. Trying to change an unwanted behavior by the enforcement of demanding, strict and confrontational disciplines cannot be achieved this way. Confrontation reinforces addiction. With such emphasis on the need to overcome addictions by sheer determination or by "thinking positively," or by scrupulously adhering to a rigid relapse prevention plan, we are drawn into an ongoing battle with ourselves, creating immense tension between our conscious will power and our unconscious programming. In a fight with ourselves, there can only be one casualty and, as a result, the addiction which is so unwanted by you, is kept constantly at the forefront of your mind. Of course, the more energy and attention given to your addiction, the more it has to remain prominent. It is a universal law ... that which you think about long enough, produces energy in the universe and if you think about it often enough and long enough, it will actually produce a physical result in your life. Simply put, *where attention goes, energy flows!*

By virtue of the same universal law, to live life forever in the belief that you need to "prevent" something, just in case it happens, is the surest way to keep it in existence. It is known as a double bind. For as long as your attention is on the need to prevent something, the something you are forever trying to prevent never goes away. It can't go away, because you have made an enemy of it and created it to be an integral part and parcel of your life. Other than your undivided attention to *prevent* that which isn't even happening, that which isn't even happening doesn't exist!

For far too long, we have all been playing out a victim consciousness, convincing ourselves that dependency and powerlessness are absolutely fundamental to the human condition. Nowhere is this belief more deeply ingrained than in the "world" of addiction and in the traditional recovery programs available to the masses. We see an obvious example of double bind in action at AA and NA meetings, where the dominant group consciousness is supporting one another to attain sobriety, but, at the same time, it is keeping a victim mentality firmly rooted in place. Although the long held view that addiction is an uncontrollable physical disease is now an outmoded understanding, there are those who still remain convinced of it.

As long as a person declares that they are "powerless" over drugs or alcohol, they remain fastened to a belief that they never stop believing. Similarly, for as long as people are professing themselves to be "in recovery", the need to be in a perpetual state of dependency never goes away. For some it is actually the inescapable dilemma of helplessness that never goes away. There is, of course, nothing at all *wrong* in maintaining such a belief. Why change anything that may appear to be working well enough? However, it is significant to realize that whenever people gather together to share their prevalent belief in helplessness and affliction, the resounding message given to head and heart is of the lower resonance of dependency and hopelessness.

While the positive intention of those attending meetings in great number is undoubtedly one of solidarity and camaraderie, the overriding group consciousness gathered there, inadvertantly feeds a victim mentality and keeps suffering in place. To go free from such a dominant "story-telling" drama of your life you must replace it with something radically different. You need something that will take you beyond the drama, so that you can see the big picture and the truth that, right now, lies hidden from you. When you awaken to that truth, you will be able to understand the true meaning of your addiction and the pain it has been masking. You will then be more consciously aware of your capacity to transcend it, taking the necessary time to heal your pain, but then also accepting that you know when it is done. The immune system of your body functions at the same level of information it is supplied. Put another way, the more you forget to re-member the truth of who you *are*, the lower your state of resonance and the more depleted your natural immune system becomes.

A lifetime spent in recovery from your addictions, with powerlessness as its overriding message, does not assist you in becoming aware and return to fullness. It keeps you in the lower state of resonance. You will have observed, that many of those committed to a lifetime "in recovery" may well be abstaining from drugs or alcohol, but are very often still not living in joy. That is because as long as you believe you are depriving yourself, or that something has had to be given up, or that you have had to learn how to go without it, you will always feel there is something missing. When too much energy is being given to what you *don't want*, only the unwanted is kept as your focus. As long as you are fixated on it your unwanted addiction literally cannot go away. It has to exist and the energy it continues to exist in, is in the form of misery. Hence the cycle of relapse ... it is not your natural state to be miserable.

> ... as long as you believe you are depriving yourself, or that something has had to be given up, or that you have had to learn how to go without it, you will always feel there is something missing.

Mainstream methods for addiction *recovery* can assist you to make adjustments to your suffering. However, they will not stir the awareness of the expansive field of *knowing* your heart has been searching. If you are to fully move out from victim consciousness and into your natural power, it is time to expand your conscious awareness and slip out from your learned dependency.

Evolution comes through conscious awareness. This is the "knowledge" that you have been missing. It is what has been missing from your attempts to recover from your addictions, just as it was missing when you became addicted. You have been remaining at a level of conscious functioning which has shown you little more than how to exist in life. If you are content to just exist, surviving your life rather than living it, then keep calm and carry on. If your heart is telling you that there must be more to your life than your experience of it has been so far, then know that your heart holds for you the innate intelligence to show you the way.

You cannot just think yourself into change. You cannot just use the same brain and the same beliefs that got you into the hole you have been in, to get you out of it. You have to move outside yourself to gain a greater perspective. Thought by itself does nothing. It's just a thought. Thought by the connectivity of emotion becomes feeling, which is an energy. Thought happens in the head. The emotion operates in the lower energy points (root) and they meet in the middle (heart), which is an electro-magnetic generator, generating energy and replenishing you. You can feel it as you do something compassionate for someone. You feel it as a physical electro-magnetic surge. That is what the heart does. It makes you feel good. It then becomes a heart-frequency and you give it out. That is how you attract into your life all that you *prefer*. This is how you will move from addiction to preference and from preference to new found acceptances about your Self and about life. This is the power of being awake, being the observer, being aware, being your Self. This is the way to stop mis-creating your life. This is the way to let go of victim consciousness. This is the way to slip out from old beliefs and repetitious thought patterns. Know it, discover how it works and allow it. That's how powerful you are!

CHAPTER TEN

Your unconscious mind

When you are inspired ... dormant forces, faculties,
and talents become alive, and you discover yourself
to be a greater person by far than who you ever dreamed
yourself to be.

—Patanjali

ALL learning, ALL behavior and ALL change is made at the level of your unconscious mind. It is one of those discoveries that really makes all the difference, once you know its significance. I'll just repeat it again, so you really grasp its importance ...

ALL learning, ALL behavior and ALL change is made at the level of your unconscious mind.

Your unconscious mind has been consistently working for you to bring about every wanted and every unwanted thing into your life, simply because that is the way you had it programmed. Not surprisingly, it's the part of your mind often referred to as your "faithful servant". Whatever it is fed, it will store as memory and will efficiently keep acting on it, with or without your conscious mind's permission. This can be as debilitating as it can be exhilarating, as you will discover.

Unless your new intention to remain free of your addictive behaviors is imbedded in your unconscious mind, you won't experience the shift you feel ready to make. It is just not going to happen. The fact that it hasn't already happened in your life, is living testimony to that.

Let me do a little explaining ...

Everyone has a conscious and an unconscious mind. One way of thinking about your unconscious mind is that it is everything you are not consciously thinking of right now. As soon as you think of something, it becomes conscious. Before that, it was in your unconscious mind. It is important to understand that your unconscious mind is the source of all learning, all behavior and all change and that it is a powerful attractor.

For you to be free of the addictions and the behaviors that have accompanied them, you are going to have to look to your unconscious mind in order to make lasting change. In short, *whatever your unconscious holds, holds you!* It will continue to attract more of the same, until it is given different programming! Let me give you a few examples of the ways your unconscious mind works and why it is important for you to get to know yours.

LEARNING. Learning is not the domain of your conscious mind. While learning must first go through your conscious mind, it is your unconscious mind that remembers everything. EVERYTHING once learned, resides in your unconscious mind.

Go ahead now and think about all the things you have ever learned. Then take some time to include all the different aspects about the addictions you have collected along the way and become so masterful at living out. Think about how practiced you became at concealing them, how manipulative you also learned to become and how secretive your actions came to be.

Now here's a thing, until I brought up the subject of addiction just there, you weren't consciously remembering from your past every single instance of your own addictions were you? On the other hand, it is not as if they had gone away, so where were they being stored when you weren't thinking of them? That's right, in your unconscious memory bank.

Think of something else, something even more routine. Think of all the phone numbers you've learned, and which you now know. Many of them may include the numbers of dealers or other people you associate with your addictions. Possibly amongst them will be contacts you've needed to avail of in times of trouble, like family members, medical services, counselors. Ask yourself again; before you were thinking of any of those numbers, where were they? Yet, as soon as you pick up your phone, you would automatically start punching in those numbers, without even having to think about them. Obviously they were stored somewhere, a place of which you were not conscious—that is your unconscious mind—the part of your mind of which you are not conscious, right now.

BEHAVIOR. All behavior is generated at the unconscious level. Even if you were to just raise your hand right now, all 159 muscles between the tip of your fingers and your shoulder blade have to be first moved unconsciously for you to make conscious movement. The same happens with walking. Do you just put one foot in front of the other? You do so without thinking about it, but as soon as you do think about walking, it becomes more difficult to do so. Thinking about walking is conscious thinking. The fact that it interferes with walking shows you that behavior is generated unconsciously. When did you last drive anywhere consciously? Do you remember the whole trip or none of it? Your unconscious behaves without you having to think about it and you'll know what I'm talking about of course. Have you ever found yourself in completely unknown territory, literally in the middle of nowhere, yet still found your way to the liquor store? Your unconscious mind is your auto-pilot! There is a downside to that, perhaps the example I've just described has in the past been one of them for you. The good news is, your unconscious mind can also be put to very positive use ... to bring about change.

CHANGE. Think now of any ingrained habit you were ready to change in the past. Was it easy for you? Probably not. Most people find it hard to change a regularly repeated behavior, believing it's something that takes a long time.

If change in your addictive behaviors was made in the straightforward conscious way you have been trying to make it in the past, you would have made it by now. Your addictions would have just disappeared the moment you made up your mind. The fact that it hasn't been accomplished that way, is because you have not been fully in rapport with your unconscious mind.

No matter how diligently you have learned about the down-sides of addiction, or doggedly attended meetings or sessions with your addiction counselor, systematically searching your moral inventory and devotedly tending to your relapse prevention plan; you will not find change possible to accomplish unless your conscious decision is in alignment with your unconscious mind.

YOUR CONSISTENT MESSAGE BECOMES YOUR REALITY. Your unconscious mind powerfully attracts! Be consciously aware. Be alert. Be definite in the messages you are giving to your unconscious mind. It will achieve for you whatever it is programmed to achieve. It never switches off. Even when your conscious mind sleeps, your unconscious mind continues to absorb information from its environment. Your consistent thoughts become your reality, as do your consistent beliefs, your consistent judgments, your consistent attitudes, your consistent behaviors.

> **Your consistent thoughts become your reality, as do your consistent beliefs, your consistent judgments, your consistent attitudes, your consistent behaviors.**

While your conscious mind takes in as much as 4 or 5 bits of new information per second, your unconscious mind amazingly takes in 2 million bits of new information per second! Relying on your unconscious mind as your "faithful servant", to achieve and to manifest for you will always be more dependable than relying solely on your conscious mind. Truth is, you are more powerfully able to attract when your conscious is in alignment with your unconscious intention.

When you wish to set your new intention, set it in the affirmative, set it as if it were happening now, in the now. You cannot NOT create, so set only the creation you would prefer to experience as your intention. Your unconscious mind loves symbolism, so paint the picture in your mind's eye of how it will look, feel and sound to be living the new-found truth of YOU, who you truly are. Make it your truth. Make it the grandest version of your greatest vision. Then relax and allow it to unfold. That is how powerful you are and that is how powerful the consistency of your intention is.

YOUR PLASTIC BRAIN. At one time it was thought that the human brain was hard-wired at birth and that, for example, you were either born smart or you weren't. However, advances in molecular biology and imaging are now giving us a very different picture. The brain now appears to be very plastic–a super sponge. It is constantly changing, adapting to and in response to outside stimuli.

Every childhood experience, every smile, bedtime story or game of peekaboo, triggers an electrical response along an infant's neural pathways, laying the foundation for future thoughts. Your childhood experiences not only influence the development of your personality, but also, your behaviors. Genes establish the framework of the brain but your "environment" quickly takes over, providing the customized finishing touches. They work in tandem with the genes providing the building blocks, as the environment creates instructions for the overall construction. This can be either a daunting or an exciting realization for you. On the one hand, it indicates that parents can't affect and influence every detail of their child's development, but, on the other hand, they can certainly provide an environment that is more conducive to the development of their child's true potential. Similarly ... just as parents have the ability to alter the structure of their child's brain, you have the same ability to alter your own brain.

From your birth, your brain is pulsing with activity as tremendous numbers of connections between neurons called synapses are formed. During the first year of life, the number of synapses jumps twentyfold from about 50 trillion to 1,000 trillion. These pathways are reinforced by what the infant sees, hears, smells, touches and tastes. Connections that are made repeatedly between brain cells are strengthened as this important neural circuitry is being laid down in the first years of human life.

Just as memory can be lost if you don't access it regularly, neuro-pathways in the brain become dormant unless they are reinforced. This is critical in the first year of development and remains important to you thereafter. The process is known as "pruning" or sometimes is referred to as "use it or lose it". Basically it means what you don't access and stimulate regularly will become dormant and inaccessible.

The implications for you as an adult, about your own continued process of development is plain to see. Just as pre-school age, when the brain is most receptive, is the time when a child learns easily and effortlessly, the adult needs to stimulate their brain when it will be in its most receptive state. Given that pre-school age has now ended for you, the nearest state of passive, timeless receptivity, free of other interferences can be achieved by entering the state of silent sitting or meditation. There are few tools more effective or more useful in achieving deep knowing, true joy and inner peace than daily meditation.

INTENTIONALLY CREATING, UNCONSCIOUSLY. Your brain is the center of your nervous system, automatically processing thoughts and allowing you to function. Your mind and what you put your mind to, is what the brain does. Your mind is your brain in action, your brain at work. Your brain has been at work, repetitiously achieving for you all that your mind has been giving it to do. Now that you have had a change of heart about what you would like your mind to achieve, your brain can get to work with its new command!

Remember, in order to make the changes your heart desires, it will never be sufficient to simply take in new information and make it understood by your intellect alone.

What you are reading in this book for example, will never bring about change if you just keep it as an intellectual exercise. Good philosophy alone does not change anything. Both your conscious and your unconscious mind need to be in rapport, actively directed towards the radical changes you wish to experience. Then you can move more naturally from your addictions to preferences and from preferences to new acceptances. Unless there is rapport between the intentions of your heart and the processing that goes on in your head, tensions between conscious willpower and unconscious programming can result in much distress. It can even lead to serious neurological disorders. Battling with the unconscious by using confrontational measures is futile. There is no use "reasoning" with the unconscious mind. Trying to suppress learned behaviors is just not going to work. A new programming is required, one that feels more right, more true, more *in tune* with your heart: more YOU.

The neuro-plasticity of your brain allows you to evolve your behaviors, so that you become more flexible, more adaptable. Neuro-plasticity is your brain's ability to change its synaptic wiring. It does that as it takes in new information and by storing it in its memory bank, unconsciously. As long as you are NOT doing that, your brain never changes. It just continues, using the same thoughts applying the old ways, no matter what new circumstances or opportunities come along. They just won't even register. You just keep on and on, living life from past memories without ever learning new things and having new experiences. Neuro-rigidity is to keep your brain firing in the same pattern and combination as it originally became programmed to do.

Every time you have a thought you make a chemical. If you have thoughts that are happy, you make chemicals that make you feel good. If you have negative thoughts, you make chemicals that make you feel bad. If you have insecure thoughts, you feel insecure and the moment you feel insecure you start to THINK the way you are FEELING ... insecure. As you do so, you make more chemicals so you can *feel* the way you are *thinking*. This of course is how the human drama unfolds. It is how you get caught in the repetitive loop that is sometimes called addiction ...

The accumulation of your thoughts create your beliefs as your beliefs create your accumulated thoughts. They, in turn, create your behaviors from which unfold your life situations. Your life situations create more thoughts to accompany your life situations, which then create more beliefs to substantiate the way you have been living ... more beliefs create more behaviors ... more behaviors create more life situations ... more life situations ... create more beliefs ... creating more of the same feeling thoughts. Your same feeling thoughts ... create your same feeling behaviors ... your same feeling behaviors ... keep your same feeling life situations, forever ongoing and always unchanging ...

Here's where that loop must necessarily be interrupted for you to reclaim your freedom from it ...

The body is to be the servant to your mind, not the other way around. The neurons of the brain possess the unique ability to store and communicate information between each other, forming a network of constant communication. As your neurons begin to form new networks, you are all the time creating a new mind through which new possibilities, new dreams, new realities can pave the way to new manifestations and experiences. You could say, this is what the brain is for!

Naturally, your brain needs to be assisted to keep that function going. It needs to be exercised, stimulated and given something new to "do", so that it can grow its new circuits and make new neurological connections. The *something* can be whatever you put your mind to. If expansion is required, then the regular message that needs to be fed to your brain must be one of expansion, so that the network of neurons can sustain and maintain the job you have assigned to it. If you forget to re-member to feed your brain cells, the regulating of your network will fall away. You are its regulator, its instructor and its constructor. The consciously aware person knows this. When you are consciously aware, your life is your message and expansion is your life. Wired by the way you live it and fired by the expression you choose for it, the neuro-network of your brain keeps the regulation of your new intentions always activated, so that there is no relapse.

Given that you lose your attention span as many as 6-10 times per minute, you can see how constant your preferred messaging needs to be—you need to live in a constant state of meditation, as the observer of yourself. This will be the way your brain *gets it!* The more consciously aware, the more you become practised at maintaining your intentionality. You see, awareness does not depend on time. When you are present, your awareness is constant. If you are in and out of awareness, consistency does not get to be built into your neuro-network. Repetition of your positive intention, is how you maintain your neurological connections. Memory is how you sustain those connections, storing your preferred intentions in your unconscious memory bank.

Remember, all learning, all behaviour and all change is unconscious. As you expand your conscious awareness, you are constantly creating or making new synaptic connections. As you remember to practise and maintain your newly created possiblities, you sustain them through your corresponding behavior. As your nerve cells fire together they wire together, building new circuits from existing ones.

Old memories can also now begin to form new memories. As you open to new possibilities, new connections are made from existing synaptic connections. Repetition of your selected new and creative information soon becomes second nature, as your unconscious mind becomes familiar with its new data. It adjusts routinely, habitually, effortlessly, easily. You can either be using your hard-wired conditioning to be creating chaos in your life, or you can be creating magnificence. But remember this ... you cannot NOT create.

In short then, you have the capacity to use your conscious awareness to expand your possibilities and your brain will do this for you. Similarly, you have the ability to not expand, to just remain exactly as you are, and your brain will also do this for you.

As you evolve, your neuro-network evolves with you!
Conscious awareness is your guide.

MEDITATION. Meditation goes to the Source. It takes you away from the level of the "problem" to the level of the solution, releasing you from dwelling in negative thoughts and dissolving old conditioning. Instead of being caught up in one issue at a time, meditation carries the whole mind beyond problems.

Begin to use meditation each day. Know that it is interrupting your relentless flow of thoughts, "messaging" every cell in your body, dissolving the energy that glues rigid habits in place and programming your new intention. With true dedication this gentle discipline can dramatically expand your consciousness over a relatively short period of time. If you have fallen out of the way of meditating, ask yourself if it is the first thing you usually drop from your routine when things get hectic. It should, of course, be the *last* thing.

Deliberately take 15 minutes in the morning and 15 minutes in the evening—more if you can find it, though not necessarily so—to be quiet with your Self ...

CHAPTER ELEVEN

Being your Self

*A man's character may be learned from the adjectives
which he habitually uses in conversation.*

–Mark Twain

There is a wonderful story told of the Buddha demonstrating the power of being more consciously aware ...

An Indian Sage once asked the Buddha:
"Are you a god?"
"No. I'm not a god," replied the Buddha.
"Well, are you an angel?"
"No. I'm not an angel."
"You must be a messiah then!"
"No. I'm not a messiah."
"Then what are you?"
"I am awake."

To be consciously aware is to be awake. To be consciously aware enables you to transcend limitations. The starting place necessary to transcend your addictive behaviors is no different from the way shown by the Buddha. It is to be awake! Becoming more consciously aware, you move from surviving to creating. Can you imagine yourself to be this change, acting with intention and knowing that the universe is in your favor? Can you create from this new starting place?

Here is a very easy way to begin the practice of being awake, so you develop the capacity to observe, to remain aware and take responsible action for your behaviors, rather than just re-acting impulsively to each passing thought and to each old belief:

WATCH ... your **W**ords
              your **A**ctions
              your **T**houghts
              your **C**haracter
              your **H**eart

WATCH YOUR WORDS. By developing your conscious awareness you observe *how* you are communicating. You develop awareness of just *what* you are communicating about yourself. Although the actual words you use in conversation convey as little as 7% of the overall communication you are making, your choice of words reflect the beliefs you hold about yourself and the judgments underlying them.

Pay attention to the words you use, either spoken or in thought. Focus carefully on what you are actually saying: *"I don't feel good today. I'm never going to make it through the day. Nothing appeals to me. Those people make me sick."* This kind of language goes on for hours, and we are often unconscious of it. When you shift your awareness away from complaining to focusing on the power and the aliveness that is within you, you will immediately shift the dense negative energy that otherwise hangs over you.

Be aware of two of the most powerful words you use: I AM.
For what you place or don't place after these two words
will limit or expand the truth of who you are ...

I am all that I say I am

If you say I AM healthy, so you are. If you say, I AM abundant, so you are. If you say, I AM happy, so you are. If you say, I AM hopeless, so you are. If you say, I AM sick, so you are and if you say I AM alcoholic, so you are.

Do not underestimate the significance of your statements, for they carry the same information to every cell in your body and hold that information there as memory. Science has discovered that we each have a "thinking" body. Every one of your 75 trillion cells "thinks" and communicates to every other cell. The implications of the power you give to words is not hard to understand and therefore, you must never underestimate their impact. They literally are the command signal that your mind and your body act upon. The more you are identifying a belief about yourself, through the words you convey, the more evidence of their powerful impact can be seen to be acting in your body.

When you say, "I am sad at heart," then you literally have a sad heart. If you were able to see inside your heart, you would find that it was heavy with sad molecules. If you say, "I am bursting with joy," then you literally have a joy-filled heart. If you were able to check your blood, you would find high levels of interleukin and interferon—powerful anti-cancer drugs—naturally being produced in harmony with your emotions.

38% of your communication is the intonation, tone, accent, rhythm, pauses and stresses of your words. A whopping 55% of all you are communicating is in the form of facial expressions, eye movements, muscle movements and the pallor of your skin as you communicate. Everything is combining to charge your words with added energy and the energy your words are communicating are affecting everything else. The 93% total of your non-verbal communication when added to the 7% of your verbal communication reveals the truth of your inner thoughts and feelings. You are always signalling a message to your mind, to your body and to others and the energy you put behind your words has

> **You are always signalling a message to your mind, to your body and to others and the energy you put behind your words has enormous impact.**

enormous impact. Your words are so often used to define who you have come to THINK you are. They often express fears of who you THINK other people THINK you are. Of course, when you are consciously aware, they can similarly be used to define *who you truly are*. Be careful then, how you are using words and at what level of energy frequency and vibration they are being conveyed.

Alcoholics Anonymous, and other such like support groups, advocate that the only hope of managing addiction is accepting that you are *not* able to do anything about them, that you are *not* able to change; that you are, in fact, *powerless to do so*. In their sort of reverse psychology, they advocate that your only hope is acceptance of your hopelessness. The paradigm here is that your greatest strength is supposed to be acceptance of your greatest weakness. By creating such a paradigm, those who teach this message then produce a need for something or someone *else* to be your strength. By admitting, acknowledging and accepting your utter powerlessness, you obtain the "power" (from another source) to change what you want to change.

Now while many claim that this approach has worked for them, it has very limited value, for it proposes a very limited view of the Self. In the bigger picture and in the long run, *that view can never be empowering*. At best, sobriety may be maintained by making the adjustment from addictive behavior, but a victim mentality and the dependency on outer circumstances remain intact and unchallenged.

Understand and accept that you did not come into this life as a victim. Nor is it necessary to be living your life in dependency in order to be the powerful presence of your Being.

If you use the incriminating words "I am an alcoholic" or even "I am a recovering addict", think again, for immediately the fearful learned version of yourself unseats the truth of your pure potential and forever locks you into that self-created helpless personality. Unless you do watch your words, the learned version of you is never over. Because your addiction has never been retired, you continue to identify with the very thing you are trying to push away. Finally, it denies you the possibility of complete and utter change. At best, you settle for a life committed to the belief and the need to remain in a perpetual state of "recovery". At worst, resignation to being rendered power-less over your challenges, can mean that you don't even get off the starting blocks.

Be careful when repeating learned thoughts and beliefs about yourself. Watch your words. Whether the belief you're carrying about your life is a truth or an untruth, your experience of it unfolds from the belief you hold about it. That's how powerful you are!

If the belief you have come to believe about yourself feels dragging, burdensome and negative, delete the belief. Go ahead right now and press the delete button, just as you can do on the computer. Now inwardly speak your truth again to your Self and reclaim your truth ...

"This is only a belief I collected along the way and which I have been using to describe myself and my life. Now that I am consciously aware of the impact and far reaching implications of my beliefs and the thoughts that have been energizing them, it's empowering to know that as I change my words I change my beliefs. That's how powerful I AM"

And breathe.

Once your truth has been re-instated and reclaimed, the belief you have been believing can dissolve. Wait for it to subside and state ...

"I am now reclaiming the truth of me from the made up belief I was carrying about me, and I go free."

And breathe.

Now declare who you truly are and use the words that more fully reflect and express that truth. Slip out from your learned vocabulary which determined your old ways of looking at life and familiarize yourself instead with words that more fully declare the unique presence of your Being. Go ahead now and practice your new-found description of your new-found Self and keep doing so until the ego gets the new message, until your unconscious mind gets the new message, until every cell in your body gets the new message and until both your head and heart are finally aligned with the *remembered* truth of *all* you truly *are*. Then *your life will be your message* and *expansion will be your life*.

WATCH YOUR ACTIONS. The actions of your thoughts and beliefs are the behaviors you begin to behave and, as a result, they are often erratic and undisciplined. So much so that in the East the expression "Taming the Monkey Mind" is used to describe the process necessary for quieting the constant self-talk that goes on in your head and which, when unobserved, similarly becomes erratic and jumpy in your actions. Like the fast moving behavior of a monkey, forever leaping from one branch to another, the ego thrives on the accumulation of thoughts and beliefs and behaves just as impulsively; acting and reacting, always "doing". Never fully aware.

Unless you are watching and aware of the thoughts that fuel your beliefs and the beliefs that fuel your thoughts, they together combine to unconsciously become your illogical and undisciplined actions. As you discover how to watch your actions, the thoughts behind them are quietened, tamed and, at once, the impulsivity of your learned behaviors is lessened.

In India, monkeys are regarded as a nuisance to the food sellers and street traders. Endearing as monkeys are to visiting tourists and sightseers, they never miss an opportunity to raid the open stalls for food or for anything else their curiosity alerts them to. Trappers, knowing that the monkeys can never resist acting on temptations, find it easy to capture them by using a weighted jar or gourd in which nuts are placed as a trap. The gourd has an opening, barely large enough for the monkey to reach its hand into, and, as it grabs the handful of bait, the monkey's closed fist does not let it get back out again. All the monkey has to do of course, is to release from its fist that which it craved, slip out from its trap and go free. The monkey however, not willing to let go, remains shackled by its resistance and is then easily picked up by the trappers instead. Impulsive, curious, impatient and acting on its one-track train of thought, the monkey serves to illustrate how our undisciplined actions become our imprisonment. Every one of your actions has its consequence. Always be aware of the behaviors you are behaving.

When you become the watcher of your actions, you will see what you are unconsciously invested in. Your conscious awareness will show you what the ego is holding onto and when its actions are leading to self-defeating results. Your made up version of yourself finds it difficult to let go because the ego has a vested interest in being right. From your place of awareness, ask yourself this question:

"Who would you be proving "wrong", if you were to let go of your addictions?"

Consider the question again:

"Who would you be proving "wrong", if you were to let go of your addictions?"

The answer to your question will give you a clue to why you have been on such a self-destructive path and why you have found it difficult to let go of it. For as long as you remain in your addictive behavior, the ego-self is proving "right" any person who may have negatively judged you in the past. If you were told how hopeless you are and how you will never make anything of your life, your repetitious addictive behavior only serves to keep their judgment of you in place. The ego is proving them *right*. If you were told that you're a loser and if you settle for their criticism, the ego is proving them *right*. If you have started to accept their judgment and have unconsciously made it your own judgment about yourself, the ego is proving them *right*.

So, in light of that ...

"Who would you be proving "wrong", if you were to let go of your addictions?"

Ponder this question in your heart, rather than in your head. Clear the unresolved matter right now between yourself and the significant other or others. Let go of another person's judgment of you by letting go of the ego's acceptance of it and you will go free.

None of what I have just said means anything of course until it is put into action. Without taking action towards the changes you desire would be like owning a wonderful new car that just sits on the driveway. You can just turn the engine and admire the hum of its motor without going anywhere. However, if you really want to discover the joy of the ride, you have to release the brake and move forward. When you put into action your desire to go free of judgment, you are completing the final stage of your empowerment. There is no better way of clearing the judgment you've been holding onto, than by using the liberating method of *Ho'oponopono* (see Chapter 3). Go ahead and clear the matter within yourself right now.

WATCH YOUR THOUGHTS. Enough said by now? Or is it ever possible to have too many reminders of the necessity to observe your thoughts.

We have to become more consciously aware of our dominant thoughts and recognize whether they are creating the energy of a positive or a negative version of life. When you become aware that you are creating a negative version of life, don't judge yourself but observe what's happening. Breathe, interrupt the thought pattern, then take a few moments to come up with a positive thought to change the direction. Sit for a few minutes holding your preferred thought, the one that's more in keeping with your *right-feeling-way-up* version of your Self. Just giving yourself time to sit with your preferred thought until it becomes your dominant thought will change your whole attitude.

The only addiction is addiction to your thoughts about some-thing. Your thoughts are a powerful magnet and you have discovered that like attracts like. To consistently dwell on all you DON'T want, all you CAN'T do and all you SHOULDN'T be repeating, is an unhelpful signal to be making to your unconscious mind, because your unconscious cannot process a negative. In fact, it's also true for the conscious mind.

> **The only addiction is addiction to your thoughts about some-thing.**

Think about this: You cannot think about what you wish to not think about without thinking about it. I'll repeat that: You cannot think about what you wish to not think about without thinking about it.

This is hugely significant to grasp and has major implications for the change you are desiring in your life ... For example, if I were to say *"Don't think about the color blue!"* What are you now thinking about? Yes, blue! Even though you were asked not to do that!!

You will have gone through your life constantly telling yourself what you didn't want to think about ... *"I don't want to be using, I don't want to be drinking, I hope I don't mess up, I can't keep getting hurt, I don't want to let people down, I'm sick and tired of being sick and tired."* All the while, you have been re-enforcing the exact opposite to your desire. Take heed. The most direct, thorough, effective and lasting change is achieved only when your unconscious mind is in alignment with the choices made by your conscious mind. The more time and energy spent in declaring what you don't want or in describing yourself in some negative fashion, the more your unconscious mind will deliver accordingly ... more of the unwanted.

Unlike the conscious mind, which rationalizes and reasons, your unconscious mind simply responds in specific detail to all its been previously given. Whatever your unconscious holds, holds you and the consistent thoughts you hold about life, your life, will be the reality you experience. So be clear, be very specific, be positive, be aligned, be consistent.

Once you become aware that you have such a powerful information processor within you, it will become your greatest ally in transcending your addictive patterns of behavior. When your unconscious mind is aligned with your new conscious intention to make change, you can also un-learn anything you have come to learn that no longer serves you well. You can undo behaviors you have become addicted to as you make the life changes you prefer. You can begin to attract into your experience the positives just

Transcending your addictive behaviors is very exhilarating. You may even think of it as your ultimate high.

as effectively as you were attracting the negative and unwanted behaviors. The difference this time, is that you are now beginning to *discover* the powerful being you truly are. Transcending your addictive behaviors is very exhilarating. You may even think of it as your ultimate high.

The more watchful you are, the more your mind starts to quieten and your thoughts start dying. They no longer have the same energy your beliefs (judgments) required. Confusion makes way for clarity and how freeing it feels to be more clear of your purpose. Your addiction had become confusion, that's why so much of it was done in secret. Your aloneness became isolation and, in isolation, your confusion became misery and, in misery, there was a profound lack of natural joy and, without the energy of joy, you became depleted, like a battery without its charger. Without energy, you became suppressed and the suppression of yourself has been keeping you small, limiting the expression of your Self. You were born with character, born unique, born with pure potential, born as Infinite Consciousness. Trying to keep the powerful magnitude of your Being confined to a very small made-up version of yourself, is not going to be possible for you to do. Eventually something has to "give".

It's often said, that for addictive behavior to change, a person must first hit "rock-bottom". But what is *rock-bottom*? For some it will be the experience of ill-health or near death. For another, it may be loss of friends, loss of loved ones. For another, it may be financial hardship. It may even take all three. *Rock-bottom* is whatever you say that you mean by it, for only you can truly assess what is working and what is not, for YOU. Which brings you to your next great discovery ...

The meaning of life is the meaning you give to it

Only when you can honestly answer *"Yes"* to the all important question: *"Have you had enough, yet?"* will you have disentangled the truth of who you truly are from the falsehood of all you had learned to become. That's how powerful this question is. Your answer to it indicates how consciously aware you have become and also just how powerful you are!

WATCH YOUR CHARACTER. Your character is not the same as your personality. Personality is a learned thing, character is the unique individuality of *who you truly are*. Character is your essence, you come with it; you are born with it. Personality is borrowed along with the borrowed attitudes, borrowed thoughts and borrowed beliefs you form *about* yourself. Your character is your Self and how you make present its essence, the essence of your Being. A child is born naked into the world and he or she is given clothes to wear to cover their nakedness. A child is born in essence, individuality, character. Unfortunately, we sometimes deliberately and often unconsciously hide that too!

Addiction is an attempt to be individual, but only knowing how to try doing so by creating a different personality. Your essence cannot be experienced that way. Watch your character, nurture it, love it back into life. For as soon as you lessen the need to present a personality to the world and begin instead to reclaim your individuality, your character will at last be made present and shine out.

Before you came into the world, you knew nothing of hatred, intolerance, racism, bigotry, indoctrination, prejudice, competition, addiction, difference or separation. For the first, most important years of your life, all you knew was what you were taught. Be careful how you are still presenting yourself in your life. If your personality has overshadowed your individuality, then call forth your essence, reclaim your character and make it present in everything.

WATCH YOUR HEART. Your head is to serve the heart, not the other way around. When you come from the heart, you are not only accessing fields beyond the physical, you are also vibrating at a much higher frequency rate. Because of that, you will bring into your awareness vastly more intelligence than your slower vibrational thought patterns were able to provide you with. The more you listen to your heart, the more you can free it by letting go of unforgiveness, resentment, unresolved hurt or the fact that you have always felt displaced in life.

Mainstream approaches to addiction treatment identify addictive behavior as a "problem" to be eradicated, squashed. It does that by searching for the causes of the problem, examines the history of the problem and then uproots the problem from its very beginning. As you attempt this process, it can cost a lot of money and time spent in therapy or, an endless sojourn devoted to being "in recovery". As a result, you end up being dragged more and more into problems behind the problem. It's insane. The thinking behind the approach is; the problem arose in the past and must therefore be tackled in the past. Trying to make possible the impossibility of your endeavor only burdens the heart. For your heart cannot be forced to keep a past alive. Your heart has moved on from it, it beats now and only now and it beats in rhythm with only that which is ever truly happening, the present.

Don't forget to remember who you are. That is all that is necessary. If it is easier to remind yourself of who you are not, then begin there, make that the starting place. You are NOT your problem. You cannot really go into the past. The past has happened. You can go to a memory of it, but you cannot go into the past. Trying to undo the past by trying to do the impossible—going into it—will only bring immense suffering. You cannot undo it to re do it. You cannot reform it. Trying to do so only saddens the heart even more, making you feel heavy hearted. The past means that all the potential of a thing is finished and your heart must be treated to the freedom of this realization.

Equally impossible is to establish the future. That also is impossible. You are not the creator of your future. You simply create, for you cannot NOT create and your creations require neither a past nor a future. The present is the only creation that can ever be in existence. It is eternally NOW and your life is not an exception. Do not waste another moment trying to make the future certain. The very quality of future is uncertainty and the past is a dead phenomenon. At most you can re-interpret past, but past remains the same. The moment you drop either one of these pursuits, you go free and your heart responds to the freedom given to it.

Addiction is a worry about the future, which never comes, a desperate attempt to hide from that which you have conjured up as being so inevitable. How have you been doing that? You went to the only place you *thought* was available to you for your verification, to the past, which does not exist. You made that which is dead the prospect for the future. Addiction is a hiding from the past, which has already become hidden from you. It doesn't exist, it cannot exist. Only the pain of trying to keep the non-existent in existence fills your present and disrupts your heart. Avoid the path that leads to the triple by-pass! How do you do that? You tend to your heart and all that it has to show you.

When you get locked into your problem, you get fixed on it. It becomes the only thing that exists for you. You identify with it totally. You speak of it as being *"my problem"*. You forget to use the peripheral vision of your conscious awareness. Because you are locked onto your myopic view of life, your life, the very direction of it makes certain things possible and absurd things also possible. You can go on and on in that direction or you can take a different starting place; a new way of looking at old ways of looking at life, your life. The moment you say, "Oops I thought I had a problem, it felt like it was *"my problem"*, it seemed like I had nowhere to go with it ... the future seemed too uncertain and the past seemed closed to me." In that moment, this "problem" cannot possibly be taken seriously, for you have brought it into conscious awareness, shed light on it, seen it for the heartache it is causing and immediately you can go free of its deceptive burden.

CHAPTER TWELVE

When you forget to remember

But always remember, you have your own Source, never leave that.

—Jelaluddin Rumi

You are now in possession of a very powerful message about life, and its primary message is this:

> *Don't forget to re-member the truth of who you are.*
> *And even if you do, there are things to re-member when*
> *you have forgotten to remember, so that you quickly*
> *bring yourself back into alignment with your Self.*

4 things to re-member,
whenever you do forget to remember

Speak them to yourself, absorb them into both your conscious and your unconscious mind, know them to be true ...

1. I am not and never can I be separated from my Source

2. I am who I say that I am

3. I cannot NOT create

4. The meaning of life is the meaning I give to it

RYAN'S STORY | "Growing up, I had an alcoholic father who was very abusive mentally and, at times, physically. Through this, I grew up in fear and with the instability of what others thought of me. I was fearful that I might not be doing the right thing or making the right decision, fearful that I was not good enough.

In my teenage years we moved a lot (not from town to town, but we were in a different house every year) and that led to a sense of never feeling settled. I have continued to feel that instability in the places I've lived since that time, in my relationships and my employment.

At the age of sixteen I left my Catholic junior school to start High school. Although I was completely unconscious of it at the time, that is when I started using alcohol and drugs to alleviate my fears and anxieties. I started spending my time with new people and stopped associating with all of my friends I had known since pre-school. Also at this same time my brother was diagnosed with diabetes, so most of my parents attention was spent attending to him. That gave me freedom to do as I pleased and I started experimenting with marijuana, hallucinogens and alcohol.

I started to get a reputation for being fun to be with and to party with. I remember at seventeen thinking I never want to give up drinking or partying, because it was so much fun! With the free rein from my parents and not getting much guidance, as I had been used to at school, I lost all other interests and just partied. Throughout this time, I was always able to hold onto my job at the local golf course and I did pass High school, but looking back I really don't know how.

When I left High school I was introduced to crystal meth and it completely took over my life. My girlfriend and I started smoking it for days on end and we would not sleep or eat for weeks. I deteriorated quickly—physically and mentally. At this point in my life I also began to gamble so that I could support my habit. I always found it much easier to be "out of it" than to deal with reality. After a couple years of this going on my parents finally started to see what it was doing to me. They decided I should go to Europe to clean up and get a new perspective on life.

I lived and traveled over Europe for two years. In that time, I managed to kick the crystal meth but exchanged it for alcohol. I found it so easy to meet and socialize with people if I was drinking, but I started to develop anxiety and panic attacks. Using more alcohol seemed to be my only remedy.

When I returned to Canada, I was lucky enough to get my job back at the golf course and I went to college and got my degree in Horticulture, majoring in Turf Management. I was then appointed as the Assistant Super-intendent of the golf course and my life was great for the next two years. I loved my work, I was responsible, goal oriented and driven. However, as time went on, I continued to drink and started gambling quite heavily. I was under a lot of pressure to marry my girlfriend at the time, buy a house and settle down. I didn't have the life skills to cope with it all and used alcohol to take my problems away. I thought gambling would also be the answer—get me the house with the white picket fence!

As my drinking and gambling got worse, I started doing cocaine and that is when my life totally fell apart. Within months I lost my girlfriend, my job and my truck. I moved to the city and started work on the oil rigs. All the time I just kept telling myself that if I made enough money, everything would be alright. However, the more money I made, the more I gambled and then I started smoking crack. I was in what seemed like an endless cycle.

I eventually ended up living on the streets with no friends, no job and no hope. There were times when I would move home with my mother, but shortly after I would start my addictive behaviors and my lying and I'd soon find myself being thrown out again.

I roamed aimlessly for five years in this state. People giving me chances and me making a mess of them. I tried everything, quitting cold turkey, 12 step programs, GA, NA, AA meetings, therapists, new girlfriends, moving to new cities but within months the same old habits and patterns would start.

Finally, one day my mom took me to see a therapist who recommended an addiction treatment center. I had struggled with addiction from my early teens and through my entire twenties. I had lived my life always running, always tired. I'd been living a life of self-destruction, addiction and substance abuse. This seemed like the only thing left for me to try. I met John Flaherty and from our first meeting things felt right. That was three years ago.

I always knew deep down that addiction to alcohol and drug use was not what I wanted my life to be, but my self-hatred and feelings of worthlessness and despair kept me on the path. I was always telling my "story" of why I was the way I was. I tried many different approaches to stop my self-destruction and nothing worked. The more I tried, the worse I felt about myself. I thought I was destined for a life of misery. I was hopeless and as I continued telling that "story" in my head and to others, the misery grew.

With John, things were different. I was able to start seeing the world through a different lens. John's message instantly made sense to me. He taught me that I am not my "story," that I am deserving of all the greatness the world has to offer. I learned that each morning I get to choose how to be "me". I can be happy, or I can be really happy! John's simple approach to life has changed my life. Although I still have my struggles, the mantras and meditation John gave me to use, as well as the ways of correcting my energy imbalance and the ways to control my self-talk, help me to stay on top of things. As long as I don't forget to RE-MEMBER, everything is well. When I do forget to remember, I also know now how to re-member the things I'd forgotten to re- member! This feels so good."

CHAPTER THIRTEEN

A leopard cannot change its spots, or can it? Changing your genes

"I could tell you my adventures–beginning from this morning," *said Alice a little timidly; "but it's no use going back to yesterday,* *because I was a different person then."*

–Alice in Wonderland

It has often been said in judgment of another, that a leopard cannot change its spots. It is a derogatory term that has possibly been used to condemn your deliberate intent to bring about radical life-changes in your own life. It is an arrogant wording, incorrectly and sarcastically used in ignorance of what more truly *is* within the natural capacity of each of one of us to achieve. The notion that things can never change their innate nature or physical appearance simply is not so. It is a belief, like many unquestioned beliefs, that has mistakenly been passed on and falsely judged to be fact. In fact, everything is changing all of the time and your biology is no exception to that universal law and fact of life.

YOUR BIOGRAPHY BECOMES YOUR BIOLOGY. Truly your biography becomes your biology and, as your biography–the "story" you tell about yourself–changes, your physical form changes in tandem with it. You literally are "different", all of the time, changed even from yesterday. Your body's rejuvenation and renewal will change regardless of your co-operation with it, but it changes even more readily and naturally when it is not having to deal with your resistance to it. Resistance to the natural order of all things changing, brings into your experience what you feel as stress and stress brings dis-ease. Without your resistance to what is, you remain free, free to evolve and to make change.

Radioactive isotope studies have revealed some remarkable evidence of our ever-changing form. We each make a new liver every six weeks, a new skin once a month, a new stomach lining every five days, a new skeleton every three months, new brain cells every year and even our DNA is changing every six weeks. Nothing remains unchanged, not even the much maligned leopard escapes the constant evolutionary cycle of change that is *life-ing* everything.

What, other than an erroneous belief, that has become a dominant thought and then a repetitious learned behavior, could possibly make you *think* your life would be such an exception to the rule? Since you, perhaps more than most, will surely be able to empathize with the sullied reputation of the poor leopard, I encourage you to take heart from all that modern day scientific studies are now revealing and, most of all, do not accept the fatalistic message of genetic determinism ...

EPIGENETICS. Biologists used to claim that we are each born with a set of genes that are fixed and unchangeable, determining our human behavior. Although this claim is now known to be nothing but theory and doctrine, many people have continued to keep it as their ill-informed belief. It is the foundational belief on which many traditional addiction treatment regimes still operate today, despite the fact that the emerging science of epigenetics has completely shattered this dogma and proven it false. You are not stuck with your genes!

The science of epigenetics, as it turns out, is showing that contrary to original claims, we actually have a tremendous amount of control over how our genetic traits are expressed. Findings have now consistently proven that there is no addiction gene determining your fate, just as for example, there is no single gene that determines your height. Rather, your genes are constantly being influenced by your environment and specifically by a complex pattern of response to the thoughts that you think, the emotions you feel, the behaviors you act and the beliefs you expect to unfold. They are also altered by the fears you possess as much as they are about the desires you long for, the relationships that you focus on and the repetitious habits you have become attached to.

While genetic factors do play a part in your development, the emphasis that has been placed on genetic influences in traditional addiction treatment processes has been misguided and is misleading. The ramification of holding onto the genetic code you were born with, and that you have learned you cannot influence, is that it leads to belief in absolute determinism. For as long as you continue to maintain such an erroneous belief, it remains an impediment to your evolution, leaving you utterly powerless to do anything about the behaviors you wish to change.

DISPELLING THE MYTH. The major problem with believing the myth that your genes control your life is that you become a victim of your heredity. It is now time for you to dispel the spell you were led to believe and to let go of its debilitating myth which has kept you locked in victim consciousness. For as long as you believe you can't change your genes, it essentially means that your life is pre-determined and, therefore, you have very little control over the health of your body. The paradigm-shattering research now referred to as epigenetics, however, reveals that your perceptions control your biology. This radically challenges the belief about inherited genes pre-determining unchangeable behaviors. Biologists have discovered that genes do not operate as previously predicted. There is compelling evidence that genes can be activated and de-activated in response to the signals received from the environment. With this new science, you find yourself back in the driver's seat so to speak. It means you can shape and direct the data of your own genetic read-out by altering your environment.

The foods you eat, the air you breathe and the thoughts you think, along with every decision and every life-style choice you make, create your "environment" and have genetic consequences. Your early environment, consisting of both the pre-natal and post-natal periods, has a profound

> **The foods you eat, the air you breathe and the thoughts you think along with every decision and every life-style choice you make, create your "environment" and have genetic consequences.**

effect on gene expression and adult expression. Your genes are being changed all of the time and they will express or suppress genetic data depending on environmental influences. While your early childhood development was greatly imprinted by the environmental influences of beliefs, thoughts and behaviors you were exposed to, the good news is; you are the one who can now control the influences that are impacting your genetic data.

You have discovered how crucial it is to WATCH your words, WATCH your actions, WATCH your thoughts, WATCH your character and WATCH your heart, and researchers have demonstrated that by regulating your life in this way, you are all the time creating the "environment" to which your genes respond.

The new science of epigenetics, proves your genetic code is not nearly as pre-deterministic as previously thought. Genes are controlled by the environment within and outside your body and, without those environmental signals, they could not function.

RE-CREATING YOUR GENETIC READ-OUT. Each cell membrane has receptors that pick up the various environmental signals they are exposed to, and this mechanism controls the "reading" of the genes inside your cells. You are not controlled by your genetic makeup. Your cells literally choose to read or not read the genetic blueprint, depending on the signals being received from the environment. So, having a family history of alcoholism or substance dependency, or being brought up in an environment where parental drug or alcohol addiction was always prevalent, does not automatically mean you are destined to inherit the same behavior. Far from it. While you may well initially mimic, as a learned behavior, the beliefs and attitudes of the family you were born into, the genetic information does not ever have to be expressed. It too can be altered. Your genetic read-out (which genes are turned "on" and which are turned "off") is primarily determined by your current thoughts, attitudes, and perceptions. The consistency of them becomes your reality.

Your emotions, which are also changing all of the time, alter your genes too, turning your genes "off" and "on" as they change. Each and every cell in your body has a type of consciousness and genes change their expression, depending on what is happening outside your cells and even outside your body. The science of epigenetics, when understood, can consciously be practised as a therapy to raise your energy vibration and to restore mental, physical and emotional equilibrium. I encourage you to in-build your therapeutic practice as an integral part of your daily routine.

Try this experiment ...

Change the environmental instructions you are giving to your cells. Simply "remind" your affected cells of their healthy function so they can go back to being normal cells, regulated *in tune* with your Self. You can begin to do this as a daily meditation, whether you are sitting or walking, regularly "messaging" the 75 trillion cells that make up your body ...

"It's natural for my body to be well.
It's natural for me to be free from all tension.
It's natural for every one of my cells to thrive.
It's natural to be at peace in mind and in heart.
I am one with my Source and all is well"

This is the process of consciously moving yourself out of victimhood and into the grander experience of *who you truly are*. It ensures that your biology—at a cellular level—is moving in synchronicity with your deliberate intent. The more you become willing to embrace this simple truth, the healthier you will become and the more automatic will be your inclination to live a lifestyle that will support your epigenetic health. That's how powerful you are!

"Our experience of addiction first arose when our younger son found himself in financial difficulty. He was taking money from our account and getting involved with banks by way of multiple accounts, overdrafts and credit cards which he had no means of repaying.

When asked about the reason for this obviously aberrant behavior the reason that was offered was that he was involved in gambling and too much unrestrained social activity. He continued his behaviors many times over the course of approximately two years. Each time he had the same "reason" and each time getting "bailed out". Each time there was contrition and remorse, with promises of it being the last time. That, however, was not to be the case.

As one might expect, the financial element was not the only issue. Other behaviors vacillating between being argumentative and pleasant, lethargic, and constantly sniffling, were also evident but we thought they may be symptoms of a possible hypoglycemic condition, which a physician had diagnosed some time earlier. Other causes we put his behavior down to were ADD/ADHD or possibly an allergy, or possibly some unknown underlying physiological or mental causative factor.

Seeking some explanation for what was evidently going very wrong, tests were arranged to try and determine if there was in fact some basis for the behavior as a result of hypoglycemia, or some unknown contributing underlying physiological or mental causative factor. The testing indicated that there did not appear to be any physiological or mental issues, so the mystery continued. Finally, under pressure from us, it came to light that the real reason for the behaviors was his habitual use of cocaine. We felt some relief for now at least there was an explanation for what was occurring and a course of action could now be taken.

Initially, given the repetitive nature of the behaviors and the deceit that had covered up the situation, we were emotionally drained and to say we found it challenging is putting it mildly. Shattering may be more accurate. The constant speculation about what could be causing such a terrible situation (the never ending WHY?) and the search for an answer took a huge toll, as did the promises that "this would be the last time" followed by yet another repetition. We struggled with the dreaded anticipation of what would be next. We knew, almost instinctively, that something else would come next, we were waiting for the bomb to drop.

When it came to light that drug use was involved, the initial fear was of the the multi-faceted damage that drug abuse can do. Immediately we began seeking assistance. It became the top priority and great effort was put into trying to find available resources.

Over the period of several months, various avenues of assistance were sought and agreed to by our son. The first step was a residential treatment program for a period of eight weeks, which proved to be of very limited value. The residential program instilled and inculcated the notion that addiction is a lifetime disease and that there would be no cure for our son. The program offered only one means of dealing with the issue and the services provided were, for the most part, meaningless. Elements of the program were arguably damaging.

It appeared that the financial interests of the organization were given inordinate priority through attempts to persuade, by what could be considered insidious means, the need for a longer stay in treatment. Objectively, at least in our view, no actual treatment was offered, but merely a slavish and zealous (almost fanatical) adherence to a portion of a traditional 12 step program. In addition, the manner in which we as parents were dealt with was utterly unsatisfactory. Shortly afterwards, a non-residential holistic treatment program was tried, but that was also of limited value.

The financial implications of our son's challenge were significant and reached into the tens of thousands of dollars, including the cost of the treatment programs. However, the real cost to us all, was emotional. We felt profoundly lost, shattered, angry, helpless, sad, disappointed. Terrible, terrifying and agonizing may be three words that sum up the experience.

Our son's return to drug use was virtually instantaneous after attending each of the programs.

At this point, the very different approach to addiction recovery of John and his wife Anne Louise Flaherty became known to us. The several days we had as a family working with them was of significant value. They immediately restored calm and inspired new hope. We came to understand that the idea of addiction as an incurable disease is misleading at best. It perpetuates the focus on fear, rather than focusing on the importance of creating a preferred alternative and a better course of moving forward.

The realization that the ability to change lies within each individual as they express a sincere desire to take a different and more preferred approach, filled us with hope. It is the difference of being able to exercise free will to overcome adversity (addiction), as opposed to being a prisoner shackled to the adversity (addiction) and remaining trapped in a constant struggle to deal with it in only one way that is, itself, tied to the existence of the addiction and depends on the constant resurrection of it.

We have come to the understanding that this way of treating addiction recovery really only substitutes one form of addictive dependency for another form of dependency ... the never ending meetings, the constant reinforcement of one not being able to make recovery on their own and the never ending reliance on others for what is truly one's own responsibility to create one's own truth (not the cookie "truth" of some program) but one's own truth. The goal for a person must surely be to come a point of being free from addictions. John explained it to us this way ...

"What has passed is now the past. The past cannot be resurrected, nor can it be changed, it simply is no more. Why? Because it is past.

There is only the present. Even in what you call the future, it will still be the present. The present is real, for it is the only thing ever present. The future is unreal, for it does not exist. The past is unreal, for it has passed. To spend time worrying about the future can only be a suffering in the present. To spend time suffering about the past, can only be a suffering in the present. Yet in the present, there is nothing ever happening, other than the thoughts and feelings you choose to fill it with. Make your preference in the now and keep choosing your preference. This is how to be present. This is how to be free." We found this message to be immeasurably powerful.

John also reminded our son how to maintain his personal peace and how to respond to others, whenever he was being pressured to live as he'd behaved in the past. He recommended this reply to those who expected him to return to old ways ... "There was a time in the past when I used to use cocaine" (*and to then tell the story of it*).........................., "but now, in the now, it's my preference to" (*and to then confidently tell of his new found life experiences*)........................

This we also found immeasurably powerful.

We were each discovering a new way of understanding life and a new way of living in it. We were realizing that desperation will not lead to positive outcomes whereas, deliberate, considered and considerate thought and intention could change everything. Some things are not always solely an individual's fault, but through personal change one, in fact, changes the world around oneself.

As a result, we have stopped panicking about our son. We do not resurrect the past which cannot be changed. We look to the present, express a preference for how life will be and take action to make that preference a reality. We are now forgiving of others and ourselves when they, or we, stumble. We try to be tolerant and understanding, not blaming. We try to allow for the differences each of us expresses without the need to have to be "right", which only feeds the ego.

Even when that doesn't come easily, we do not give up. If necessary, we fake it until we make it. Without forgiveness, we know that blame continues and blame is predicated on resurrecting the past and making it the present which only perpetuates the problem.

Anne Louise explained to us that "What you resist persists." So we've given up our blaming and let it go—it is the past. We can learn from the past but it cannot ever be the present, unless we fill the present with it. Prior to our time with John, the feeling of guilt and of having done something wrong to cause our son's drug use was overwhelming. The need for the always elusive answer to "WHY" we were all having this experience was like a crucifixion, one nail after another. We are all the better for having undertaken the journey of Self-discovery with John. It was such a positive relief from what had been experienced before. It frankly put all that had passed before in the name of treatment to shame. The experience has been life changing and life affirming for us all as a family. We know we will have to work at it, but we now know how to do that. We have a new way of looking at ourselves, others and the world. We know that addiction is not an incurable disease. Nor is it a life- sentence to some form of purgatory. There is light at the end of the tunnel for us as a family. Our son's challenges have opened the way to our own train to freedom, Self- actualization and truth. We have a MUCH MUCH GREATER APPRECIATION OF LIFE!

What John helped us to accomplish in a few days was not, and would never be, achieved through any other mechanism or self-styled "treatment program". If you are reading this and find yourself in a similar situation with a worry about your own son or daughter, do not wait to find yourself in the position of saying "If only someone had told me", or, "If I had known at the start what I know now", because now you do know. While this may sound somewhat zealous, it is actually an objective and perhaps even restrained endorsement of the value of what John and his wife Anne Louise have brought to all of us."

CHAPTER FOURTEEN

For all those affected by the addictions of their loved ones: parents, partners, siblings, children and friends

The Teacher is one who hears you and then unveils you to yourself.

—Ibn Arabi

It is more than likely that you chose to read *Addiction Unplugged: How To Be Free* in order to get into the "mind-set" of a loved one, someone you desperately want to assist. It is quite possible that it was you who found this book, in the hope that your loved one would actually be the one to read it. That may or may not happen but, one thing is for certain, this book has made its way into your hands and not by any accident. The liberating message of these pages is now being addressed to you. I do encourage you to share its message with others, but only after first absorbing all that its truth has to bring to your own conscious awareness.

As you recall the *4 Things to Re-member, when you forget to remember*, know that you are all the time diminishing the old ways of looking at your life and paving the way for change.
Speak them again to yourself now ...

1. I am not and never can I be separated from my Source
2. I am who I say that I am
3. I cannot NOT create
4. The meaning of life is the meaning I give to it

Other people in your life are only ever providing situations where things that are hidden within you can be experienced. They are not the cause of them. If the behaviors of another person are directly affecting you; unsettling you, worrying you, frightening you, threatening you, challenging you, then they are there for you to discover truths about yourself that could never have been made possible without their disturbance.

The other person, is simply providing a situation in which emotions hidden in you can come out in the open. They are reminding you of who you are NOT, so that you may discover the truth of *all you truly are!* Whenever this happens, remain centered in the inner feeling that this is just so. Surrender to the realization this truth holds for you and begin your own discovery of everything about your Self you would have missed, had it not been for their disturbance.

You are not and never can you be separated from your Source. Know in your heart and in your head that whenever life looks like it is falling apart, it is really just falling together. The old is giving way to new, as it does all of the time. Only your non-acceptance of that truth brings you suffering. Life changes all of the time and, for as long as you are connected to your Source, your individual experience of it is always being newly re-sourced with every breath in and with every breath out. Life isn't judging you, it has no agenda. Only your reaction to another, through the thoughts you think, the emotions you feel and the judgments you make, have the capacity to disturb you and the potential to bring about immense suffering.

You are who you say that you are and, your reaction to others, is indicative of how well you have come to know your Self. Observe your reactions, watch them, remain alert, be consciously aware. Are you trying to live the made-up story of someone else, or are you the one who is consciously aware that there is a drama unfolding in another person's experience?

Adding to the *story* of another person's drama, does not lessen the pain of it for them or for you. Judging their *story* does not lessen it. To belittle the *story* of another, does not make it disappear. Loving acceptance of another, without equating it with a *story* of your own or with one of theirs, is sufficient. Love their Being as you learn to love your own. Their behavior, no differently from your own, is the drama their accumulated thoughts and emotions have created as their *story*. They have learned to tell a very dramatic *story*, possibly a very disturbing *story*. You have contributed to their *story*, as they have to yours, for you cannot NOT create. Now create from your place of conscious awareness ...

Close the mind-made difference the fear-filled ego-self has conjured up, telling you that there is a divide between you and your loved one. Clear the past in the present. For the past *story* of another does not exist in the present, unless of course you continue to create it there. I remind you once more of the powerful means to dissolve the disturbance that your mind-made difference is causing you ...

"Thank You"

As you feel the disturbance of your loved one's *story* arising within you, know that it is actually your own disturbance that you are now feeling. You will feel it within your mind and within your body, for that is where it resides. Feel it, until you heal it. Sit with its discomfort until it dissolves. Your own inner disturbance has been there for some time without you being consciously aware of it, accept that. Your loved one has stirred it again within you, and dramatically this time, so that you may now fully re-solve it. That is how life works and that is how powerful you are! Keep speaking the words *"Thank You"*, in grateful recognition for this freeing discovery.

'I'm sorry, please forgive me"

We each have so much power inside but so little knowledge of how to use it. Real power comes from knowing who we are and what our place in life truly is. It lies deep within us. It is the power with which you were born.

When you feel that you have got lost in your own or, in someone else's *upside-down* version of life, or when you feel overburdened or overwhelmed by the disturbances your loved one is bringing up in you, know that you have temporarily forgotten to re-member all that you are. Remember that your power comes from knowing that everything is just as it is and that everyone involved is unfolding in the drama exactly as they are supposed to do. As you speak the words, *"I'm sorry, please forgive me"* you are reminding yourself of your forgetfulness. It is your *upside-down* version of yourself, the ego-self that you are forgiving. At once your *right-feeling-way* up Self, your character, your essence, the power of who you truly are, can reclaim its more rightful place. You will feel its calm presence, as soon as it has been reclaimed.

"I Love You"

As you speak the words *"I Love You"*, it is neither the ego-self in you, nor the ego-self of the one creating disturbance, that you are addressing. Rather, it is your acknowledgment that love will replace fear as you return yourself to your Self.

Fear is a most expensive emotion to entertain, as also is worry; so expensive are they that you simply cannot afford to entertain them a moment longer. Fear attracts fear, just as, by a different attitude of mind, you invite and attract the influences and conditions you desire.

The "world" of addiction and of addiction treatment and recovery has created an environment where fear remains dominant all of the time. It is vital to *slip out* from such a fear-filled version of life, if you wish to be free of its negative affects on you.

You will have noticed that the "world" of addiction recovery has its own jargon. It may even have become a jargon you have started to use in your own expressions. Terms like *"overcoming"* or *"beating"* addictions, *"being on and off the wagon"*, *"getting your shit together"*, *"facing your demons"*, *"fighting the beast within"*, *"slaying the dragon"*, having *"a monkey on your back"*, or *"the devil on your shoulder"* ...

It's a peculiar "world" that has been created, don't you think? Its language, and the imagery conveyed, is sensationalist. It instills fear and gives far too much dramatic and fanciful attention to that which you DON'T WANT to expend your energy. It only serves to make the unwanted all too prominent and gives it far too much credence. You can't afford to be spending any more energy on that which you want to bring to an end. It's now time to unplug that which has been consuming all your energy. It is time to re-direct your own conditioned attention and focus, just as much as it is for your loved one to re-direct theirs.

You can't afford to be spending anymore energy on that which you want to bring to an end. It's now time to unplug that which has been consuming all your energy.

You have the power to make new appearances replace old ones. You do that by calling forth, from the heart not the head, a new state of being. The words *"I Love You"* bring closure to that nightmarish world you had become lost inside. Let love now dissolve the nightmare that you had made so dominant.

Know this ...

People in close relationships usually have the same issues, but in reverse. For like attracts like, in an "opposite" way. For example, if you struggle with love, you'll attract someone who has mirror issues with love. If you believe that only "tough love" will make a difference, know that you too will feel the effects of that difference. For in order to demonstrate toughness you must first toughen up. Do you really want to make yourself tough in the hope of giving and receiving the peace you actually desire? There is no such thing as *tough love*, there is only love. How tough you make it, is reflective of only how tough you have found it is to receive it. I suggest it is just another example of the unhelpful jargon that belongs to the "world" you are now ready to *slip out* from.

There are many more examples of like attracting like, in an opposite way ... In a relationship where one dominates, the other will be passive. If one partner is caught up in addictive behaviors, the other may be a rescuer. If each share fear, one may be drawn to experiences of risk-taking while the other prefers to keep both feet firmly on the ground. Neither of you will necessarily like the other's way of experiencing life, yet, in a sense you are perfect for each other. One person's more direct approach to a perceived "problem" may push all the buttons of another, while the other's refusal to deal with it may actively push theirs.

One thing is for certain ... for everything to change, all you need to do is to change everything. This time around, however, the only change you need to make is change within yourself. It is in fact, the only change you possibly can make. That's how powerful you are!

The meaning of life, is the meaning you give to it and here is a great statement for you to make as you begin each new day. You will find you will be able to make this statement a more truly reflective belief, as soon as you can stop judging the differences your loved one stirs up in you ...

Everything in life is perfect,
I have no complaint whatsoever.

You have no idea how powerful that statement is. Speak its truth to yourself, even if you have not yet learned how to believe it! If you were to say it 300 times in a day, until you come to believe it, it would still not be too many. I can only leave it for you to make your own discovery of its efficacy in your life. If you are to be accused of going into denial as you do so, I suggest it is a denial that is well worth making. For you are denying everything your head would convince you is so separate between you and your loved one, for a belief your heart already knows to be true.

Life is forever moving you toward the completion of your Self. It naturally moves you toward any healing necessary, after deep hurt has been your experience. Only the ego can experience suffering, by clinging onto the false identification it has mistakenly assumed for itself.

Your true Self, knows nothing of suffering, because it has nothing invested in the drama of the "stories" made up about yourself or about another. However, before you can experience the freeing discovery of giving yourself back to your Self, life will deliver everything unlike itself to your doorstep for healing.

For example, if you ask life to make you more loving, don't be surprised if it brings hard-to-love people into your life. Only by first experiencing the contrast of that which you desire, can all that you desire be recognized by you. Remember, if you hadn't first experienced hot, how would you know cold and, similarly, if life were only to send you more easy to love people, how would you ever know how to love?

Once this new dawning becomes your new discovery, you will at last realize why the addicted person is so prominent in your life and why your unwanted experience of their behavior has been so difficult to shift. The disturbing behavior of your loved one will remain the experience you are experiencing in your life, only for as long as it takes you to discover the reflective truth of that disturbance, which already exists within you.

I best repeat that one again, for you can't afford to miss its truth, it is a truth that sets you free ...

The disturbing behavior of your loved one will remain the experience you are experiencing in your life, only for as long as it takes you to discover the reflective truth of that disturbance, which already exists within you.

This is for your own discovery ...

The behavior of the one you love is simply mirroring your own inner disturbance. Fear attracts fear. For as long as the ego is competing against, and in conflict with, the

The behavior of the one you love is simply mirroring your own inner disturbance.

ego in another person, it is fear that you are each living, not love. What you thought was love, is really only fear, fear that there may not be enough of all that you both crave ... love itself.

Healing of a relationship begins as soon as you let go of the beliefs (judgments) you once so doggedly held onto. The mind-made separation between yourself and your loved one then begins to close. As you make your own inner peace with yourself, the life-changing process of giving yourself back to yourself begins to take root. The behavior of another, no matter how testing it once was to you, will no longer push the buttons of your own vulnerabilities. Your loved one, whose ego-self seemed to be so difficult for you to tolerate, has brought into your conscious awareness a most precious gift. Their disturbing presence has remained prevalent in your life to remind you of who you are NOT, so you may discover who you truly are. You are in their life so that they similarly may make their own Self-discovery. That is what love is and your acceptance of this discovery is how to be free.

As we each discover how to *slip out* from the suffering our unawareness has been causing us, we go free. Without our reaction to other people in our life, we no longer have the same *story* to keep telling about it. What was once the insurmountable drama we thought it so necessary to be giving our full attention to, now disappears. For without our full attention and our every reaction to it, a story can never become the perpetual drama we otherwise turn it into.

Once a person is encouraged to get in touch with and express their deepest feelings in the secure knowledge that they will not be rejected, criticized, nor expected to be different, a re-arrangement or sorting-out process often occurs within the mind which brings with it a deep and lasting sense of peace. Love has the capacity to instill that inner peace of heart and mind in another, just as it has to settle distubance within yourself. Judgment is never required.

"Thank You" ... "I'm sorry, please forgive me" ... "I Love You".

"I am a father with two grown children and a busy career. Like all parents, I had hopes and dreams that my children would find careers that challenged them, friends that supported them, a partner that complemented them, and generally find their own way in the world.

My daughter moved from where we lived in Canada to the US, where she continued her career after graduating from University. She has always been very focused and knows what she wants in life. She has grown into a strong intelligent woman.

My son moved away from home to go to school in Vancouver and later to work. He worked in a restaurant and the routine was to work late, in a fast paced, high pressure environment, and later to wind down by having a few drinks. This pattern lead to him drinking quite heavily. I was providing him with a low level of financial support but over time he began asking for more and more money, more than should be necessary for normal expenses. When I pressed him on this issue, he said that he had been using cocaine to get "up" and sustain, then alcohol to wind down and sleep.

This was my wife's and my first exposure to addiction and we were not well equipped to cope with it. We argued about how to handle our son. Should we just cut off all financial support? If we did that would he end up on the street? Should we somehow get him into addiction counseling or even rehab? How do we do that when he lives in another city? We both had our individual doubts and guilt that there was something we should have done differently when he was younger. Our relationship suffered as we tried to manage normal life and work. We just hoped that something would change in our son's life, that somehow he would pull himself out of what we saw as a deep hole.

For his part, my son created his own story of his circumstances that freed him from ownership and accountability. He often called asking for money. Each individual request was plausible, but collectively adding up to us supporting his dependency. I am sure that anyone, not as emotionally involved as we were, could have seen this. We shared little of this with our friends because we also knew that what we were doing was not helping him to make change. Nonetheless, we were afraid of what the alternative might be.

Over a two to three year period my son struggled with addiction. My daughter lived away and my wife and I struggled to cope with the tension that was building between us. Guilt and fear both played a part. It all bottomed out when my wife unexpectedly took her own life. Words cannot express the shock, pain, guilt and devastation that myself, my son and my daughter experienced. We each tried to cope with her death in our own individual ways and together as a family, but we failed and each of us withdrew into our own pain.

Shortly after my wife had passed away, my son's addictions spiraled out of control and I assisted him to enter a private addiction facility in Canada. He entered a ninety day addiction program and this is how he came to meet John Flaherty. My son spoke very highly of John and found some hope in John's approach. He began at last to deal with the problems he had struggled with for the past few years.

When my son left the addiction facility he began to work with John on a regular basis. Eventually it made sense for both of us to seek the assistance of John. I needed help to resolve my own past issues and assistance to come to terms with my wife's passing. I also required John's mentoring in order to build a better understanding of my son. In time, my daughter also became involved and we were able to move forward together.

Prior to talking to John I had felt that my son's problems were somehow of my creation and I believed that part of my role as a parent was to fix him in some way. My inability to do that led to frustration, despair and a feeling of helplessness. For a three year period no interaction with my son had ever been without stress. My marriage was a casualty of this situation. The only time in this period that I ever relaxed was during his stint in rehab and this was not because I held out hope that he would be "cured", rather it was because I knew that someone else was actively supervising him. It wasn't my role in that period and, as a result, I didn't feel that I was failing at it for a window of time.

With both my son's struggles and those of my wife, I found that the medical system is not user friendly or even useful when it comes to dealing with mental health issues. Finding help is not easy. I've been in emergency rooms, addiction clinics, psychologists' offices and psychiatrists' offices. The addiction clinic that costs $30,000 for a 90 day session freely admits that the number of people who leave there and relapse is "most". Only a minority turn their life around.

Living with loved ones who have addiction issues and the underlying root causes of their addiction is isolating and debilitating. It can be a cycle of ups and downs. Hope builds as things improve only to be dashed again as your loved one fails to meet your expectations yet again. There are many books and resources that outline the impact clearly and exceptionally accurately. Surprisingly, there seem to be no resources that tell you how to dig out from under that burden and get happiness and hope back into your life.

John's unique message is about understanding what you are doing to yourself and then changing it. It is about improving your relationship with yourself. It has little to do with the success or failure of your loved one's struggle, although it impacts how you react to it. In my case it has improved my relationship with my son dramatically.

John's early discussions with me explored how I was living my life reacting to my son's struggles. He also helped me see how I was basing my decisions on what I thought was expected of me.

I was raised in a traditional Scottish-Canadian family where I was taught that you did what had to be done and you did what was "right". You worked hard. Complaining was a waste of time. As the man of the house, your family was your responsibility no matter what. Your reputation and your word were the most important thing you had. You didn't ever air your dirty laundry in public. So, when my girlfriend got pregnant we got married because I couldn't fathom any other option. I will always remember my father's best friend telling me on my wedding day "today you proved you are a man!"

My father came to Canada with little money and to no job. He never finished school because he had to go to work full time when his father died (he was the oldest child). When the union went on strike a year after he got his first job, he went out and found another job so he could support my mother. I loved my father and used him as my role model and tried to make my own life work in the same way.

Using that model, my son's addiction issues were my responsibility. Yet realistically, they were out of my control. I was doing things because I was worried what other people might think of me. It now seemed like I was failing in life, despite having been married for more than thirty years with a successful career and having ensured that my children received a good education.

When I met John I was hoping that he could help me "fix" my situation. That I could somehow change my son with his help. I learned instead over a fairly short time, that I needed to treat myself, not my son.

Initially this was disappointing because my perception at the time was that I was not the "problem". I could not grasp that making changes in myself could possibly alter the circumstances of life around me. However, I began to realize that I had been very hard on myself and that in order to make any progress in my relationships, I had to first forgive myself. Intuitively, this makes sense because when my son failed to live up to my wishes for him and fell into addictive behaviors, it was emotionally crushing ... not for him, only for me. With that in mind, it made sense to try John's approach.

John introduced me to the ancient tradition of *Ho'oponopono*, which I initially thought was just an interesting discussion. However, as I tried the approach of stopping when I was upset or stressed and focusing on myself, I found that I began to feel better. The practice of "Thank you, Please Forgive me, I'm Sorry, I Love you", although a little "mystic" sounding at first, actually helps bring a great calmness.

I learned that I was very hard on myself for past mistakes, when in many cases I was incapable of making any other decision than the ones made at the time. I felt it was my fault that my son had addiction issues. As his father, I should have done something different raising him. I had deep guilt about my wife's death and I felt that my two adult children blamed me for her death.

Another truth that John helped me with was even more basic. He said, "You need to understand that what other people think of you, is none of your business. It's their problem, not yours." As strange as this may sound it is incredibly liberating. I realized that much of the time my actions were governed by my concerns about what I thought other people expected of me. This was rooted of course in the way I was brought up, but the impact it had was that I was not always doing what I thought was best. Rather, I was doing what I thought my family and friends expected of me.

The most significant breakthrough for me was that learning to listen to my feelings, learning to forgive myself and learning to act without dwelling on what other people might expect, could make a profound impact on those around me. My relationship with my son improved. We built trust and respect for each other. I began to act positively rather than defensively. I helped my son find an apartment and helped him find some stability, rather than trying to fix his issues for him.

I have stopped trying to fix my son's problems. He still has struggles. I love him and support him and try to be positive in all my dealings with him. I believe that he knows that and thus we are closer now than we have ever been. My advice to others would be that you can choose how you see the world and thus you can choose how you act in it. If you act positively, you will make a positive impact on your own life and the lives of those you love."

CHAPTER FIFTEEN

Putting it all together: powering up

We are not human beings having a spiritual experience.
We are spiritual beings having a human experience.

–Pierre Teilhard de Chardin

"*Where are you going?*" asked an Eastern pilgrim on meeting the plague one day. "*I am going to Baghdad to kill five thousand people,*" was the reply. A few days later the same pilgrim met the plague returning. "*You told me you were going to Baghdad to kill five thousand people,*" said he, "*but instead, you killed fifty thousand.*" "*No,*" said the plague. "*I killed only five thousand, as I told you I would; the others died of fright.*"

Fear is the emotion which creates chaos in our lives, the mind-made illusion that we are separate from our Source. Fear is not the same as caution which keeps us safe and is the body's natural protective reflex in dangerous situations. Fear can paralyze every muscle in the body, it hugely impacts our health and is always exaggerated by our thoughts. There is nothing to be gained by it, but everything to be lost.

VICTIM CONSCIOUSNESS. It is fear that initiates addictive behaviors and fear that keeps them repetitiously playing out in the ego-drama that unfolds. Yet the drama can always be interrupted, once we are more consciously aware. Let me give you two imaginary examples. The first reveals how deceptive the ego-self can be, while the second reveals just how fragile the ego's grip actually is ...

You arrive at work one day, only to find through the grapevine that your company is downsizing. No one can tell you that your job may be at risk, but it might be. From the ego-self, your fears, based on past judgments about yourself, immediately kick into *monkey mind* reaction:

"I could lose the one thing I really need just now. They know I've taken time off work in the past when I was drinking heavily. They know I'm still seeing the Counselor. They're sure to release me this time around. I need this job to support myself. I'll never get another one like it. They may not even give me a reference. If they do, it will be terrible. I can't believe I've let this job have such control over me, but I have. I gave it everything and now I have nothing. I'll never make anything of my life. I know I'm a loser, but I really don't deserve this. Life always has that nasty habit of biting me in the back-side when I'm just doing well. I know exactly what my father will say when I tell him this."

These are typical fear-filled thoughts, generated by the ego, when you find yourself in crisis. They are negative, blaming, judgmental, critical, frantic, condemning and they are totally invested in a power outside of you. This is victim consciousness.

In truth, what really is being threatened here is not the loss of a job, but loss of control. The ego, fearing loss of control, leaves you to believe that you are separate from your Source, that you have got something wrong, that life is as good as over, that you will never get another chance. It is precisely this kind of situation that is likely to trigger in you the fear that nothing ever changes and that your future is going to be nothing more than a re-hash of the worst of your past experiences. This will be the time, of course, when you are most likely to return to the same soothing methods you relied on in the past; drugs or alcohol. In actual fact nothing is really happening in this situation. Your thoughts, however, are already convincing you otherwise and so the punishing inner conflict begins.

RE-CLAIMING YOUR SPIRITUAL POWER. Now let's reframe the situation, from the more consciously aware perspective. The more consciously aware you become, the more you dis-identify from thoughts, emotions, and reactions. THIS IS NOT THE SAME AS DENIAL. It is more a case of "re-organizing" the way you see and feel and are in life. Your sense of self—of who you are—undergoes a shift. Before you were re-actions. Now you are the awareness. There's a world of difference ...

You come to work to find that the company is downsizing, and the following opens up to you:

"I've complained every single day since I started this job, I have obviously brought something in my reality to a head here. Whatever happens, happens, so let's see what next experience life is already making the way for. I know things always work out. They've always been very understanding of me when I've taken time off work. If I do move on, I'll see what this time in my life has all been for. I've certainly grown in confidence, since the days when I was drinking so heavily. Times like these used to really trouble me in the past, but I've now come to realize that when life may often look like it's falling apart, it's really just falling together. The last time this happened, I had no idea that this place of work even existed. My life is unfolding, as it always is, and I'm already getting a good feel for whatever changes are ahead. It's another opportunity for me, because I know that in any event, the externals will also fall into place as they need to. Whatever happens, I know I can't be hurt."

You can see immediately that unplugging from the first scenario and plugging into the second brings a far greater sense of security. This is so much more than positive thinking. This is to live your life in alignment with life itself. Reality shifts as you shift. The more consciously aware you are, the more at one with life you are. There can be no separation between you and your Source, for you are life and life is YOU.

> **Reality shifts as you shift. The more consciously aware you are, the more at one with life you are.**

Even in the midst of the most threatening of fears, the consciously aware person comes to know that there is still a point, somewhere within, that remains absolutely untouched. Not even death itself can touch it. Without giving any attention to it, allow whatever fear that has entered your awareness to pass completely through you like a wave. Only your attention to it makes it REAL. Without your attention, it cannot exist, for you have given it no power.

The more relaxed you are, the more the still point within you will become very evident, in contrast to the fear that is outside of you. You may gain a sudden insight or inspiration. You may start to feel more centered; sudden spurts of energy or alertness may occur. Be open to whatever comes. You are now finding how to relate to awareness itself, the purest level of experience. At the same time, you begin to dis-identify with the ego's total fixation on keeping everything under control, and make a shift in perception that will dissolve even the most in-dissolvable of fears. *Slipping out* from the repetitious loop of ego-driven thinking, you literally drop the victim mentality of being powerless and you drop the mind-made belief that life is up against you. Watch the body. As you watch, be indifferent to it. There should not be any tension in you. Without tension, fear disappears automatically. Once you have the knack of it, you will soon *discover* that if you are relaxed, fear cannot get attached to you.

DYING BEFORE YOU DIE. The Sufis, who are the Muslim mystics from the Islamic tradition, have a well known term for the process of becoming more consciously aware. They describe it as *"dying before you die"*. By that, they mean to literally "die" to the falsehood of your thoughts, and the fears that accompany them, before it is actually time to physically die.

Think of the number of times you have gone back into your addictions, after a period of not being absorbed by them. Your first reaction is one of fear, soon followed by shame or guilt, judgment, anger or sadness. What has been done cannot be undone, but it can be re-solved differently.

In the past, you would have been overwhelmed by your negative self-talk and all the fearful implications your thoughts bring up for you. The ego-self would either have spent a whole lot of time feeling helpless, plunging you into guilt, or, in kamikaze fashion you would have doggedly kept going in self-destruct mode until your addictive behavior exhausted you, brought you to a stop.

HOW TO BE FREE. I have shared with you an entirely new way of observing your life by re-membering the truth of *who you are*. Now you can watch whatever is happening outside of you and become consciously aware of all that can differently be directed from inside of you. This is how to stay in alignment with the Source of life that is sourcing you. This is how to maintain your personal peace and move through the challenges that used to frighten you so much in the past.

This is how to be free ...

1. Acknowledge that you have momentarily forgotten to re-member the truth of *who you are*.

2. Return yourself to your Self, not spending a second in judgment of the past.

3. Make the grander expression of your Self fully present, and decide what that means for you.

In fact, everybody becomes more consciously aware at some point, it is just a question of how long it takes you. The quicker you re-member to slip out from the ego-self and back to the powerful truth of who you truly *are*, the less your suffering will be. Life is a process of *discovery*, remember? Your desire to be free from your addictive pulls and the fear-filled thoughts and self-deprecating judgments underlining them, has brought you to a time in your life where you are ready to expand. You have been looking for YOU and life has brought you every experience and every opportunity to satisfy that craving, so you may discover the *truth of all that you are*.

CHAPTER SIXTEEN

Nothing external can have power over us

If we can only realize at heart what one's true nature is, one then will find that it is infinite Wisdom, Truth, Bliss, without beginning and without end.

–Ramana Maharshi

We have simply forgotten to remember that we all have locked deep within us a spiritual power that holds the key to our freedom. Nothing external—nothing existing as effect— can have power or authority over us.

Close your eyes and say "I". Then remember that at six years of age you could have closed your eyes and said "I", in exactly the same way in which you are saying it now, and it would have been the same "I" that you are talking about at this moment. Get in touch with that "I" now, feel your connectivity to it. That "I" has never changed, and it will never change and never die. That "I" is your Being, your true Self, your character, the Infinite Consciousness that you are. Everything other than that "I", is the ego; that which you have conjured up *about* yourself. It is who you have learned to become.

As we are born into this life, the ego-identity is formed. As we leave our bodily existence, the ego is also left behind. Life, however, never dies and as you become more consciously aware of that truth, you will know that the "I" you have always been connected to, is the the same "I" you can never be disconnected from. The "I" will have simply *slipped out* from the fearful, limited, ego-self you had learned to create and once thought yourself to be.

In transcending your addictions, you are literally dying to *who you had learned to become*. As you free yourself from every authority that once controlled your life, the "I" reclaims its more powerful presence.

I have a few people to thank. My gratitude and love goes first to my wife and soul mate, Anne Louise, for believing in me and giving me total support for writing this book, even when times got hard. My gratitude to her is boundless, for she has been with me throughout my own life-changes when I needed her most. She has also taught alongside me, inspiring people to make major life-changes in their own lives from the liberating message we share.

This book of course could not have been written, were it not for the very many people who are ready to embrace its life-giving message and transcend their addictive behaviors. Some of those, now living the message of this book, have kindly offered to contribute the remembrances of their own personal "story" for inclusion in these pages: Jordan, Dorian, Pardeep, Nicole, Matty, Ryan, Clare and Richard, Jim. I thank each of them for their heartfelt honesty, sincerity and willingness to share their accounts, so that readers may be heartened and encouraged by them to transcend their own addictions.

I thank every other person, scattered across the world, whose lives we have been able to touch; many of whom continue to passionately share their new-found definition of *who they truly are*, with those who are ready to be enriched by the same discovery. May they continue to grow and to expand in conscious awareness, and may their lives be a powerful presence, wherever they stand.

I thank those who supported the launch of this book with financial backing, making it possible to extend the message of *Addiction Unplugged: How To Be Free* to a far greater readership ... Nicole Karam, Clare Zupan and Richard McNally, Miles MacDonald, Steve and Billy Richardson, as well as those who made anonymous donations.

I owe a special debt of gratitude to my nephew Thomas Gray, who lovingly and meticulously designed the artwork and layout of this book. I also acknowledge my niece Katie Gray for her careful editing, reviewing, proof-reading and suggestions for last minute improvements.

My love and gratitude to my mother and my father for choosing to have me and for accepting my request to incarnate through them. My gratitude too, for every single one of my life experiences to date. Every experience has its purpose. Who are we to judge the "good" ones from the "bad"; all are life's opportunities to expand.

Finally, love and gratitude to my three year old great nephew Aidan, who has never been too far away from me as I have been writing. Aidan is still only three years removed from the purity of his original Source. That's a short enough length of time to have not yet forgotten the Source from which he came, yet long enough in human form for the ego-self to be emerging. If you were to take a religious perspective, you might say Aidan was as near to "God" as he could ever be. If you were to take a scientific description of him, you might say that every atom and molecule and particle and even the space between was pure potential. His timely presence in my life encapsulates everything that is contained in the message of this book. It is the same message that is so powerfully and succinctly announced by Christ when he said:

"Truly I tell you, unless you change and become like little children, you will never enter the kingdom of heaven." (Mt 18:3)

You see, Aidan is able to teach every adult how to be free and how to make life *heaven on earth*, for he hasn't yet learned how not to be free. He has no regard for the past. For no matter what wonderful experience adults may have treated him to yesterday, that which is not happening now, in the NOW, is not given a moment's consideration. Time means nothing, no-thing. Future does not exist. Worry has not yet been taught to him. No shame, no guilt. Everything is an opportunity for play. He can use his imagination to be anybody he wants to be. He will assign adults the role he wants them to play: "Just do it!" ... then the game of life commences.

Nothing is impossible. Lack does not exist. If he does not have the props required, he simply adopts the attitude of "Let's pretend". There is wonder in everything new. There is no difference between real and unreal. No inhibition. No problem. There is caution, but no fear. I acknowledge Aidan's invaluable contribution to my life, assisting me, as he has, not to forget to re-member ... That's how powerful "I" am!

Life is a game; play it
Life is a challenge; meet it
Life is a dream; realize it
Life is love; live it

Sathya Sai Baba

John Flaherty is an experienced Teacher of Spiritual and Emotional Wellbeing. An expert in the field of addictions, he has inspired people in many different parts of the world to be free of their addictive behaviors and to live a more fulfilled existence.

John began his career as a Catholic Priest, but after 11 years he made a life-changing decision to leave the priesthood and to begin his own personal journey of Self-discovery, Self-awareness and Self-empowerment. Further academic studies gained him a B.A Honors in Theology from Leeds University, England and a Masters in Drug & Alcohol Policy from Trinity College, Dublin, Ireland. Searching always for the most effective and progressive tools to move beyond limiting beliefs and fears, John became a Master Practitioner of Neuro-linguistic Programming (NLP), Time Line Therapy and Hypnosis and then gained certification as a Master Practitioner and Trainer of Meridian Energy Psychology.

Dedicated to assisting others to transcend their own challenges of life, John's life journey has taken him from England to Ireland and to Canada, where in both the statutory and private sectors he established and managed innovative projects and psychotherapy services for those addicted to alcohol and substance use, for the care of those affected by HIV/AIDS and for the emotional care of families and loved ones.

John has developed his own unique and powerful approaches for raising the human spirit and for more than 25 years he has been inspiring and mentoring each person to find emotional freedom, increased confidence and personal peace.